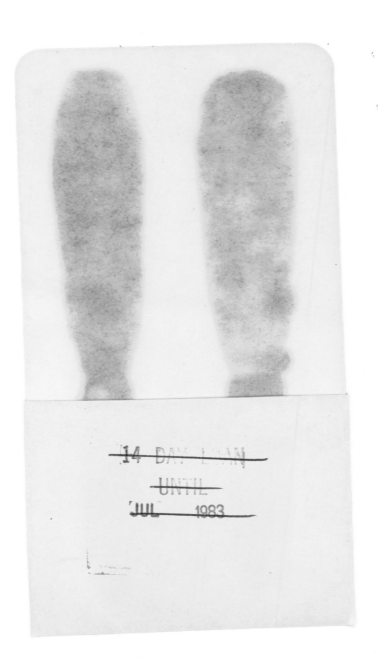

The Romanov Family Album

Introductory text
Robert K. Massie

Picture research and descriptions
Marilyn Pfeifer Swezey

Assembled by Anna Vyrubova

The Vendome Press
New York   Paris

Edited by Alexis Gregory and Daniel Wheeler
Designed by Marlene Rothkin Vine

First published in 1982 in Great Britain by
Allen Lane, an imprint of Penguin Books Ltd.

Published in the United States of America and Canada by
The Vendome Press, 515 Madison Avenue, New York, N.Y. 10022
Copyright © 1982 The Vendome Press, New York, N.Y. 10022
Illustrations © Yale University, New Haven, Conn.
Quotations from Anna Vyrubova's *Memories of the Russian Court*
courtesy Macmillan and Co., © 1924

Distributed in the United States of America by
The Viking Press, 625 Madison Avenue, New York, N.Y. 10022
Distributed in Canada by Methuen Publishing Co.

Library of Congress Cataloging in Publication Data
Vyrubova, Anna Aleksandrovna, 1884–
The Romanov family album.
　　Bibliography: p.
　　I. Nicholas II, Emperor of Russia, 1868–1918—Family—
Iconography.　　2. Nicholas II, Emperor of Russia, 1868–
1918—Iconography.　　3. Alexandra, Empress, consort of
Nicholas II, Emperor of Russia, 1872–1918—Iconography.
I. Title.
DK259.4.W97　　　947.08'3'0924　(B)　82–7098
　　　　　　　　　　　　　　　　　　　　　　　　AACR2
ISBN:　0–86565–019–5
Printed and bound in Italy by
Grafiche Editoriali Ambrosiane SpA, Milan

Contents

Introduction

"I see wonderful things!" exclaimed British archaeologist Howard Carter when he first poked his head into Tutenkamen's tomb and there, by the light of a flickering candle, glimpsed the glitter of golden objects that had slept for thirty centuries. Something of the same feeling came over me the first time I saw the collection of Romanov photographs from which the present series has been selected.

My wife and I found them almost by accident. In the autumn of 1966, I was nearing the end of three years' work on *Nicholas and Alexandra*. Suzanne, long involved with the research and editing, had taken complete charge of the search for illustrations, scouring commercial film libraries and seeking individual pictures in private hands. At the time, she was also writing frequently about ballet and had become a friend of Evgenia Lehovich, the director of the School of American Ballet. Evgenia and her husband Dimitry both were interested in our attempt to re-create the life of the last Russian Imperial family, and Evgenia suggested that I might like to meet a Russian friend of theirs, Sergei Taneyev, who lived in New York. Taneyev was the brother of Anna Vyrubova, the intimate friend and confidante of the Empress Alexandra; perhaps, Evgenia suggested, he could add something to the story his sister had told in her book *Memories of the Russian Court.* I was eager, but Mr. Taneyev, it developed, was not; he had apparently tired of being identified as "Anna Vyrubova's brother." But he did say to Evgenia Lehovich, "Tell Mr. Massie that Yale University has some of my sister's things."

I reacted casually to this information. After telephoning New Haven, where a charming Research Librarian named Marjorie Wynne confirmed that Yale did, indeed, have certain materials catalogued only as "Romanov Memorabilia," I arranged to go up and take a quick look on Saturday morning before attending a football game. I had been writing myself into exhaustion; an afternoon in the fresh air seemed a healthy prescription.

And so, on an October morning in 1966, Suzanne and I walked into Yale's Beinecke Rare Book and Manuscript Library. We met Miss Wynne and filled out the required forms. Soon, from behind closed doors, a small, rolling table was wheeled in, laden with six fat albums in cloth and leather, all peeling and cracking at the edges. We opened the first album. Here were photographs of an Edwardian family in the lighter moments of life. But, incredibly, they were not just any Edwardian family; they were the Russian Imperial family, which a few years later would be obliterated in the revolution that obliterated so much of the life and culture of Old Russia. Turning the pages, we found hundreds of pictures, collectively confirming the millions of words I had read about the life of this couple and their children. It was an extraordinary collection: the most complete set of intimate photographs of the Imperial family to survive the holocaust of the revolution. Not only had most images of this kind been lost, scattered, or confiscated during the revolution itself, but afterwards there were stories of attempts by Soviet agents to locate, remove, and destroy from all public and commercial archives any photographs depicting the last Tsar and his family as normal human beings whose faces and activities might arouse a shred of interest or sympathy.

But here they were, like Tutenkamen's treasure, miraculously surviving. We have them today because of an unusual set of circumstances. The years when these pictures were taken coincided with the first days of the age of popular photography. The capturing of images on a light-sensitive surface was half a century old by the turn of the 20th century, but it was during the prewar years of the Edwardian era that amateurs began regularly to take informal pictures—we call them snapshots—of family and friends, on guard and off. Kings and Queens, no less than noblemen and middleclass folk, issued the command, "Look this way! Now hold very still!" pointing their Brownies at each other.

Nicholas II had an especially keen interest in photography. It was he who commissioned the extraordinary collection of early color photographs of the Russian Empire by Sergei Prokudin-Gorskii, a collection that has recently been published. Traveling for six years across the expanse of Russia, Prokudin-Gorskii took pictures of rivers, lakes, and forests, of simple wooden churches and thick-walled fortress monasteries, of muddy village streets and everyday peasant life, of canals, locks, and bridges, and brought them back so that the Emperor could see his Empire. Naturally, like most monarchs of the day, Nicholas II also employed official court photographers who recorded the ceremonial scenes of pomp and flourish which went with the specialized work of royalty. In addition, however—and this is where we today are extremely fortunate—Nicholas kept some of these photographers on assignment even when he and his family were off-duty; now the cameramen's task was to capture moments of intimate family life. And so the shutters clicked while the Emperor went rowing, finished a set of tennis, or strolled off into the woods in search of mushrooms. They recorded the Empress knitting on her yacht or wading barefoot along a rock-strewn beach. They caught the little Tsarevich Alexis playing soldier and teasing his kittens. Sometimes, the cameras were, in fact, held by royal hands—several of the pictures in this book were taken by Empress Alexandra herself.

Once the films had been processed, duplicate prints were delivered to the Imperial apartments. There, after dinner, the family hugely enjoyed settling down to an evening of pasting pictures into green leather albums stamped in gold with the Imperial monograph. After 1907, the Empress' closest friend, Anna Vyrubova, joined the intimate circle. She too had copies of the prints, and she arranged and captioned them in her own albums, even as the Empress was doing the same beside her. Nicholas stood nearby, supervising the placement and mounting of the photographs and always insisting that the work be done with painstaking neatness. "He could not endure the sight of the least drop of glue on the table," wrote Anna later. How faithfully she followed his instructions is apparent to any visitor to Yale.

For most people picking up this album, I think it is safe to predict that the central figure in these photographs will be the Tsar (or Emperor: both titles are correct), Nicholas II. This descendant of Peter the Great and Catherine the Great was the last Autocrat of all the Russias, a terminal status for which he has borne a heavy weight of historical judgment. His deep religious faith mingled with an excessive fatalism; the one gave him strength, the other hobbled initiative. "I have a firm, an absolute conviction that the fate of Russia—that my own fate and that of my family—is in the hands of God who has placed me where I am," Nicholas declared. "Whatever may happen

left: The Emperor, Nicholas II, on board his
yacht, the *Standart.*

right: The Empress Alexandra on her terrace
at Livadia in the Crimea.

to me, I shall bow to His will with the consciousness of never having had any
thought other than serving the country which He has entrusted to me." Noble
as a private creed, this declaration was an inadequate definition of leadership,
and Nicholas, his family, and Russia paid a terrible price. But in these pictures
we see Nicholas in a different set of roles: as devoted husband and father, as
a charming, gentle man, and a strong Russian patriot. This is a *family* album;
here is the Tsar as a *family* man.

   Fewer people will be drawn immediately to Alexandra, but for me she is
the figure of primary interest. Considered a great beauty in her youth, she
appears here as a severe, melancholy woman whose sad expression is only
rarely softened by a hint of a smile. (My favorite is the photograph of the
Empress and her daughter Olga on page 42 in which both are struggling
unsuccessfully to suppress evidence of glee.) In general, smiles seldom
appear on these pages, because Russians, then and now, do not beam as
Americans do each time the photographer commands. Indeed, Russians
rarely smile at all in public and not often on greeting someone new, an
occasion when Westerners consider a bright expression an act of simple
politeness. Russians do not smile unless something is funny, and then,
usually in private, they grin from ear to ear and shake the walls with laughter.

The Empress is magnetic to me because she emerged as the pivotal figure in this family which stood at the summit of government and society in Imperial Russia. Who was Alexandra Feodorovna? Born Princess Alix of Hesse-Darmstadt in 1872, she was a granddaughter of Queen Victoria, the child of the old monarch's second daughter, Princess Alice, who had married Louis IV, Elector of Hesse. Alix therefore grew up in a household where English influence was overwhelming. Portraits of Queen Victoria, Prince Albert, and the English cousins hung in the drawing rooms and hallways; staircases and bedchambers were lined with sketches of English scenes. An English governess, Mrs. Orchard, had been imported to rule the nursery, where she ordered simple English meals for her charges, making certain that baked apples and rice puddings appeared regularly. Even Christmas dinner began with a goose and ended with plum pudding and mince pies specially brought from England.

In 1878, when Alix was six, diptheria ravaged the Hessian house, carrying away first Alix's sister May and then her mother, Princess Alice. The death of her mother had a powerful effect on the six-year-old child. She sat silent and withdrawn in her playroom while her nurse wept in the corner. Suddenly, all the toys were new; the old familiar ones had been burned as a precaution against the disease. Although hot-tempered and obstinate, Alix had been a merry, generous, and sensitive child. After this tragedy, she began to seal herself off from people, hiding her affections beneath a hard shell of aloofness. She grew to dislike strange places and to avoid unfamiliar people. Only in the bosom of her family where she could count on warmth and understanding did Alix relax. There the serious, cool Princess Alix became once again the cheery, dimpled "Sunny" of her early childhood.

After her daughter's death, Queen Victoria kept a close watch on little Alix. Governesses and tutors in Darmstadt were required to send special reports to Windsor, and the Queen wrote back pages of advice and instructions. Under this tutelage, Alix's standards of taste and morality became thoroughly English and Victorian. She loved English chintz and later in Russia decorated her rooms—aboard the Imperial train and yacht as well as in the palaces—with these bright floral patterns.

Alix of Hesse first met Nicholas Romanov in 1884 when she was twelve and he was sixteen. The occasion that brought them together was the marriage of her older sister Elizabeth (called Ella) to his young uncle, Grand Duke Serge. He admired her looks and gave her a brooch, but she was shy and flustered and handed it back. Five years later, when Alix was visiting Ella in St. Petersburg, she met the Tsarevich again. By this time the Heir to the Russian throne was a slender young man with blue eyes and a quiet, gentle charm. "Nicky smiled his usual tender, shy, slightly sad smile," wrote a cousin.

Nicholas did not forget the tall, blue-eyed Princess with red-gold hair, but his daily life was filled with frivolous distractions. Having been well drilled in languages, he spoke French and German passably and English like an Oxford man. He rode, danced, drank, and shot like a royal Prince. For a while, his interests also included a seventeen-year-old dancer in the Imperial Ballet, a small, vivacious girl, with a supple body, full bosom, arched neck, dark curls, and merry eyes, who had set herself to captivate the Tsarevich. She succeeded and for a time she and Nicholas shared a house in St. Petersburg. But dancers were youthful wild oats; Nicholas' real love was elsewhere: "My dream is to marry Alix H. [of Hesse]," he wrote in 1892. "I have loved her a long while and still deeper and stronger since 1889 when she spent six weeks in St. Petersburg."

The suitor did not find it easy to persuade either his parents or his beloved. Tsar Alexander III and Empress Marie had hoped for something more substantial than this minor German Princess. But Nicholas insisted that he would marry no one if he could not have Alix.

The moment of decision arrived in the spring of 1894 during the ceremonies surrounding the wedding in Darmstadt of Alix's older brother. It was as if a royal trumpet had blown, summoning crowned heads and titles from across Europe. Queen Victoria, then seventy-five, was there, along with her son, the Prince of Wales, and her grandson, Kaiser Wilhelm II of Germany, and other Princes, Grand Dukes, and lesser royalty. Nicholas had come to represent his ailing father, Tsar Alexander III, but he devoted his whole energy to the pursuit of Alix. On the second day Nicholas wrote to his mother: "We were left alone and with her first words she consented. I cried like a child, and she did too, but her expression had changed. Her face was lit by a quiet contentment." A cousin recalled: "I was sitting in my room getting ready for a luncheon party when Alix stormed into my room, threw her arms around my neck and said, 'I'm going to marry Nicky!'"

That summer the young couple spent six weeks together in England. They went to a cottage at Walton-on-Thames belonging to Alix's eldest sister, Princess Victoria of Battenberg. For three days they lay on the banks of the river, walked on the green lawns, and gathered fruit and flowers. Under an old chestnut tree in the garden, they sat in the grass, and Alix embroidered while Nicholas read to her. "We were out all day long in beautiful weather, boating up and down the river, picnicking on the shore. A veritable idyll," Nicholas wrote his mother. Years later, the mere mention of those three shining days at Walton was enough to bring tears of happiness to Alix's eyes.

All too soon, this idyll was crushed under the weight of events. Nicholas returned home from England to find his father gravely ill with nephritis. Alix was sent for and arrived just in time to see Alexander III die at forty-nine. As the guns of the warships in Yalta Harbor thundered a salute to the new Emperor Nicholas II, the twenty-six-year-old autocrat tearfully asked his brother-in-law: "Sandro, what am I going to do? I know nothing of the business of ruling."

Amidst the funeral candles and chanted litanies, Princess Alix, now converted to Russian Orthodoxy and given the new Russian name of Alexandra Feodorovna, was suddenly to be married. Nicholas' uncles felt that marriage would help calm the shaken, neophyte monarch. "One's feelings one can imagine," she wrote her sister. "One day in deepest mourning, the next in smartest clothes being married…a white dress instead of a black." Nevertheless, on her wedding night, before going to bed, Alexandra wrote in her new husband's diary: "At last united, bound for life, and when this life is ended, we meet again in the other world and remain together for eternity." The next morning, she wrote again: "Never did I believe there could be such utter happiness in this world, such a feeling of unity between two mortal beings. I love you, these three words have my life in them."

In November 1895 a first child—a daughter, Grand Duchess Olga—was born. Three more daughters arrived at two-year intervals: Tatiana, Marie, and Anastasia. Then, on 12 August 1904, a fifth infant was born, and Nicholas wrote in his diary: "A great never-to-be-forgotten day when the mercy of God has visited us so clearly. Alix gave birth to a son at one o'clock. The child has been called Alexis."

Only six weeks later, a shaken Emperor wrote again in his diary: "Alix and I have been much worried. A hemorrhage began this morning without the slightest cause from the navel of our small Alexis. It lasted with but a few interruptions until evening." Medical specialists arrived, only to offer a grim diagnosis. Alexis, like his great-uncle Prince Leopold of England, his Prussian cousins, and eventually his cousins, the royal Princes of Spain, had hemophilia. As the years went by, this illness and its effects on the boy's parents would cast a long shadow over Russia.

Meanwhile, Nicholas and Alexandra had established their winter home at Tsarskoe Selo. Located thirteen miles south of St. Petersburg, this suburban town surrounded and served two Imperial residences: the great Catherine Palace built by Peter the Great's daughter, the Empress Elizabeth, in memory of her mother, Catherine I; and the smaller, more modest palace built by Catherine the Great for her favorite grandson, who became Emperor Alexander I. These palatial residences stood in a vast scenic park brightened by an artificial lake and studded with architectural curiosities—ornamental bridges, a Chinese village, a replica of a mosque, sham ruins, all typical of the "picturesqueness" demanded by the 18th century taste for so-called "English gardens."

Tsarskoe Selo was a special world of its own. Members of the nobility and officers of the Tsar's household regiments lived in the town, occupying fashionable villages as well as modest houses surrounding the Imperial park, which remained open for all to enjoy. It was not unusual for nannies, escorting their charges along the paths, to encounter the Empress taking her children for an outing on foot or in a carriage. Tsarskoe Selo had its own famous lycée for the children of town families. Its alumni included Pushkin, for whom the town was renamed after the revolution.

Arriving in Tsarskoe Selo, the young Emperor Nicholas II and his wife chose the less ornate Alexander Palace, a graceful yellow-and-white building designed in the classical style. In the wing of the palace reserved for the private apartments of the Imperial family, the Empress decorated the rooms mostly in her favorite bright English chintzes. Nicholas' office was off the parlor, a small room with plain leather chairs, a couch, a desk, a bookcase, and a table spread with maps. The bed chamber was larger. Here, between

The Catherine Palace at Tsarskoe Selo, as photographed by the Empress.

tall windows looking out on the park, stood a large double bed, which the Emperor and Empress shared for twenty-three years. Next to the bedroom Alexandra had her famous mauve boudoir. Everything in it was mauve: curtains, carpet, pillows. Even the furniture was mauve-and-white Hepplewhite. Books, papers, and porcelain and enamel knickknacks cluttered the table, while icons covered the walls. Over her chaise longue the Empress hung a picture of the Virgin Mary. A portrait of her mother, Princess Alice, looked down from another wall, and on a table in a place of honor stood a large photograph of Queen Victoria.

In this room where she felt secure, the Tsaritsa spent the best part of her day. In the morning, propped up with pillows on her chaise longue, she read, knitted, or wrote letters. Nicholas, who always rose early, dressed by lamplight, and disappeared into his office to work, would appear in midmorning to drink a glass of tea and talk with his wife. They spoke to each other in English. As in the days of their courtship, he was always "Nicky" to her; to him, she was "Alix" or "Sunshine" or "Sunny."

Next to the mauve boudoir was the Empress' dressing room, containing an array of closets for her gowns, shelves for her hats, and trays for her jewels. Often it was Grand Duchess Tatiana who came to comb her mother's hair and pile the long red-gold strands on top of her head. When almost dressed, the Tsaritsa summoned her maids to fasten buttons and clasp on jewelry. She preferred pearls to all other jewels, and several ropes of pearls usually cascaded from her neck to her waist. For daytime, Alexandra wore loose, flowing clothes trimmed at the throat and waist with lace. She considered the famous "hobble skirts" of the Edwardian era a nuisance. In the evening, the Empress put on white or cream silk gowns embroidered in silver and blue; she wore them with diamonds in her hair. Because of her height, Alexandra insisted on low-heeled, pointed shoes, usually bronze or white suede. Outdoors she carried a parasol against the sun, even when wearing a wide-brimmed hat.

A new lady-in-waiting, recalling her presentation to the Empress in the garden at Tsarskoe Selo in 1907, gives a vivid first impression: "Advancing through the masses of greenery came a tall and slender figure....The Empress was dressed entirely in white with a thin white veil draped around her hair. Her complexion was delicately fair....her hair was reddish gold, her eyes...were dark blue and her figure was supple as a willow wand. I remember that her pearls were magnificent and that diamond earrings flashed colored fires whenever she moved her head....I noticed that she spoke Russian with a strong English accent."

For the children of the Imperial family, winter was a time of interminable lessons. Beginning at nine in the morning, tutors drilled them in history, geography, arithmetic, Russian, French, and English. Still earlier, however, they submitted to examination by Dr. Eugene Botkin, the court physician, who came daily to look at throats and rashes.

When the weather was good, the Tsar and his children suspended work every morning at eleven and went outdoors for an hour. Sometimes they climbed into small rowboats and cruised through the canals that criss-crossed the Imperial park. Nicholas had a kennel of eleven magnificent English collies and enjoyed walking with the dogs frisking and racing about him. In winter, he joined the children in shoveling snow, cross-country skiing, sledding, and building the traditional Russian "ice mountains" found in every village, big mounds of snow covered with water which froze and made a handsome run for sleds and small toboggans.

Although dinner at midday was the ceremonial meal at Tsarskoe Selo, neither Nicholas nor Alexandra cared for rich, complicated dishes. Fresh caviar had once given the Tsar severe indigestion, and he rarely ate this supreme Russian delicacy. Most of all, he relished the simple cooking of the Russian peasant—cabbage soup or *borsch* or *kasha* (buckwheat) with boiled fish and fruit. Alexandra cared nothing for food and merely pecked at anything set before her.

In the afternoon, while her children continued their lessons, the Tsaritsa often went for a drive. The order "Prepare Her Majesty's carriage for two o'clock" stimulated a burst of activity at the stables. The carriage, an open, polished black rig of English design, was rolled out and the horses harnessed into place, while two footmen, in tall hats and blue coats, mounted the steps in the rear. The coachman—a tall, heavy man in an immense padded coat— gave the reins a flick, and, with a single mounted Cossack trotting behind, the carriage set out.

At four, the family gathered for tea. Small, white-draped tables were set with glasses in silver holders, plates of hot bread, and English biscuits. Cakes and sweetmeats never appeared, and to Anna Vyrubova, Alexandra complained that "other people had much more interesting teas." Although she was Empress of Russia, wrote Vyrubova, she "seemed unable to change a single detail of the routine of the Russian court. The same plates of hot bread and butter had been on the same tea tables...[since the days of] Catherine the Great."

As with everything else at Tsarskoe Selo, there was a routine for tea. "Every day at the same moment," Anna Vyrubova recalled, "the door opened, the Emperor came in, sat down at the tea table, buttered a piece of bread and began to sip his tea. He drank two glasses every day, never more, never less, and as he drank, he glanced over his telegrams and newspapers. The children found teatime exciting. They dressed for it in fresh white frocks and colored sashes, and spent most of the hour playing on the floor with toys. As they grew older, needlework and embroidery were substituted. The Empress did not like to see her daughters sitting with idle hands."

After tea Nicholas returned to his study. His work habits were solitary. Unlike most monarchs and chiefs of state, he had no private secretary. He preferred to do things for himself. On his desk he kept a large calendar of his daily appointments, scrupulously entered in his own hand. When official papers arrived, he opened them, read them, signed them, and put them in envelopes himself. He once explained that he placed things exactly because he liked to feel that he could enter his office in the dark and put his hand on any object he desired.

The Emperor received visitors informally. Standing in front of his desk, he gestured them into an armchair, suggested that they might like to smoke and lighted a cigarette himself. He was a careful listener, and although he often grasped the conclusion before his visitor had reached it, he never interrupted.

At eight, all official interviews ended so that the Tsar could go to supper. Nicholas always terminated an audience by rising and walking to a window. There was no mistaking the signal, and newcomers were sternly briefed to withdraw, no matter how pleasant or regretful His Majesty might seem. "I'm afraid I've wearied you," Nicholas would say politely, breaking off conversation.

Family suppers were informal, although the Empress invariably appeared at the table in an evening gown and jewels. Afterward, she went to

On the Baltic shore at Peterhof are the Grand Dukes Oleg and Constantine, sons of the Grand Duke Constantine, the Tsar's uncle, and Anna Vyrubova surrounded by the Tsar's daughters (standing from left) Tatiana and Olga and (seated from left) Anastasia and Marie. Anna, as usual, is holding her camera.

the nursery to hear the Tsarevich say his prayers. In the evening after supper, Nicholas often sat in the family drawing room reading aloud while his wife and daughters sewed or embroidered. His choice, said Anna Vyrubova, who spent many of these evenings with the Imperial family, might be Tolstoy, Turgenev, or his own favorite, Gogol. On the other hand, to please the ladies, it might be a fashionable English novel. Nicholas read equally well in Russian, French, and English, and he could manage in German. His voice, said Anna, was "pleasant and [he had] remarkably clear enunciation." Books were supplied by his private librarian, whose job it was to provide the Tsar each month with twenty of the best books from all countries.

The end of these pleasant, monotonous days arrived at eleven with the serving of English tea. Before retiring, Nicholas wrote in his diary and soaked himself in his large, white-tiled bathtub. Once in bed, he usually went right to sleep. The exceptions were those occasions when his wife kept him awake, still reading and crunching English biscuits on the other side of the bed.

The second floor of the Alexander Palace contained the nurseries. In the mornings, Alexandra could lie back on the chaise longue in her mauve boudoir and through the ceiling hear her children's footsteps and the sound of their pianos. In their large, well-aired rooms, the four Grand Duchesses were brought up simply, sleeping on hard beds without pillows and beginning each day with a cold bath. Olga, the eldest, was most like her father. She was shy with long, chestnut-blond hair and blue eyes set in a wide Russian face. She read widely, both poetry and fiction, and spoke intelligently, with frankness and wit. Mostly, however, she was remembered for her kindness to others and for the depth of her private feelings. In June 1914, there was talk of a match between Olga, then eighteen, and Crown Prince Carol of

Roumania. "I don't want it to happen," Olga fiercely declared. "Papa has promised not to make me, and I don't want to leave Russia. I am a Russian and I mean to remain a Russian."

Tatiana, eighteen months younger than Olga, was closest to their mother. The tallest and most elegant of the sisters, Tatiana had rich auburn hair and deep gray eyes. She was energetic and purposeful: "You felt that she was the daughter of an Emperor," recalled a Guards officer. If a favor was needed, all the children agreed that "Tatiana must ask Papa."

Marie, the third daughter, was the strongest and most conventionally beautiful of the four. She had pink cheeks, thick, light-brown hair, and dark-blue eyes so large that they were known in the family as "Marie's saucers." In adolescence, she was merry and flirtatious. Her first cousin, Louis of Battenberg, who would grow up to become Earl Mountbatten of Burma, watched her at family gatherings in Germany and declared later that at the age of twelve, "my dream was to marry her." Indeed, Marie herself—whom everyone called "Mashka"—loved to talk about marriage and children.

Anastasia, the youngest daughter, was a short, blue-eyed child renowned in her family chiefly as a wag. When the saluting cannon on the Imperial yacht fired at sunset, Anastasia liked to retreat into a corner, stick her fingers into her ears, widen her eyes, and loll her tongue in mock terror. Anastasia also had a streak of stubbornness, mischief, and impertinence. The same gift of ear and tongue that made her quickest to pick up a perfect accent in foreign languages also equipped her admirably as a mimic. Comically, sometimes cuttingly, the little girl aped precisely the speech and mannerisms of her elders.

Cloistered at Tsarskoe Selo without a normal range of friends and acquaintances, the four young Grand Duchesses were even closer to each other than most sisters. Olga, the eldest, was only six years older than Anastasia, the youngest. In adolescence, the four proclaimed their unity by choosing a single autograph, OTMA, derived from the first letter of each of their names. As OTMA, they jointly gave gifts and signed letters.

Rank meant little to them. They worked alongside their maids in making their own beds and straightening their rooms. Often they visited the maids in their quarters and played with their children. Within the household, the Grand Duchesses were addressed in simple Russian fashion, by their names and patronyms: Olga Nicolaievna, Tatiana Nicolaievna, etc. When addressed in public by their full titles, the girls felt embarrassed. Once at a meeting of a committee for which Tatiana was honorary president, a noblewoman whom the girls knew intimately began by saying: "May it please Your Imperial Highness...." Tatiana stared in astonishment, and when the Baroness sat down, the Tsar's daughter kicked her violently under the table. "Are you crazy to speak to me like that?" she whispered.

In the Alexander Palace the two oldest girls shared a bedroom and were known generally as "The Big Pair." Marie and Anastasia shared another bedroom and became known as "The Little Pair." Gradually, as they grew up, the sisters made changes in their spare surroundings. The camp beds remained, but icons, paintings, and photographs went up along the walls. Dressing tables and couches with green-and-white embroidered cushions were installed. The young women gave up cold baths in the morning and began taking warm baths at night with perfumed water. All four girls used Coty fragrances. Olga preferred *Rose Thé;* Tatiana favored *Jasmin de Corse;* Anastasia stayed faithfully with *Violette;* and Marie, who tried many scents, always came back to *Lilas.*

opposite above: The Grand Duchess Tatiana with the cannons at Peterhof.

opposite below: The Grand Duchess Marie in the garden at Livadia.

right: The two youngest Imperial children, the Tsarevich and the Grand Duchess Anastasia, on the terrace of the Old Palace at Livadia.

As Olga and Tatiana grew older they played a serious role at public functions. Although in private the girls still referred to their parents as "Mama" and "Papa," in public they spoke of "the Empress" and "the Emperor." Each of the two Grand Duchesses became Colonel-in-Chief of an élite regiment, and wearing its uniform with a broad skirt and boots, the honorary commander attended military reviews sitting side-saddle on her horse. Escorted by their father, the pair began attending theatres and concerts. They were also allowed to play tennis, ride, and dance with eligible young officers, but always carefully chaperoned. At twenty, Olga obtained the use of part of her fortune and began responding to appeals for charity. Seeing a child on crutches while she was out for a drive, Olga inquired and found that the parents were too poor to afford treatment. Quietly, the Grand Duchess put aside a monthly allowance to pay the bills.

The youngest child of this tightly knit family was a handsome little brother with blue eyes and golden curls. "Alexis was the center of this united family, the focus of all its hopes and affections," wrote Pierre Gilliard, a Swiss tutor who became very close. "His sisters worshiped him. He was his parents' pride and joy." From the beginning, Alexis was a happy, high-spirited infant, and his parents never missed an opportunity to show him off. When the baby was only a few months old, the Tsar met A.A. Mosolov, director of the Court Chancellery, just outside the nursery. "I don't think that you have yet seen my dear little Tsarevich," said Nicholas. "Come along and I will show him to you."

"We went in," said Mosolov. "The baby was being given his daily bath. He was lustily kicking out in the water.... The Tsar took the child out of his bath towels and put his little feet in the hollow of his hand, supporting him with the other arm. There he was, naked, chubby, rosy—a wonderful boy!"

The Tsarevich after a severe attack of hemophilia, his bent left leg in a brace as a result of severe bleeding into the joints.

The combination of exalted rank and hemophilia guaranteed that Alexis would grow up under a degree of care rarely lavished on any child. While he was very young, nurses surrounded him every minute. When he was five, his doctors suggested that he be given a pair of male companions and bodyguards. Two sailors from the Imperial Navy, Derevenko and Nagorny, were selected and assigned to protect the Tsarevich from harm. When Alexis fell ill, they acted as nurses. "Derevenko was so patient and resourceful that he often did wonders in alleviating pain," wrote Anna Vyrubova. "I can still hear the plaintive voice of Alexis begging the big sailor, 'Lift my arm,' 'Put up my leg,' 'Warm my hands,' and I can see the patient, calm-eyed man working for hours to give comfort to the little pain-racked limbs." For months after a very serious bleeding episode, Alexis' limbs and joints would remain abnormal. Several pictures in this collection clearly depict a flexed left knee resulting from a severe hemorrhage into the joint which had not yet been fully reabsorbed.

For weeks, sometimes months, Alexis seemed as well as any child. By nature he was as noisy, lively, and mischievous as Anastasia. While a toddler, he liked to scoot down the hall and break into his sisters' classroom, interrupting their lessons, only to be carried off, arms waving. By the age of three or four, he would often make impromptu appearances at the dinner table, going from place to place to shake hands and chatter with each guest. Outdoors, he peddled around the park on a large, specially constructed tricycle, built to look as much as possible like a normal bicycle.

Within the family the Tsarevich obeyed his older sisters and wore their outgrown nightgowns. Nevertheless, outside the family, Alexis understood that he counted for more than his sisters. In public, it was he who sat or stood beside his father. He was the one greeted by shouts of "The Heir!" and the one whom people crowded around and often tried to touch. When a deputation of peasants brought him a gift, they dropped to their knees. Told that a group of officers of his regiment had arrived to call on him, Alexis interrupted a romp with his sisters. "Now, girls, run away," the six-year-old boy said. "I am busy. Someone has just called to see me on business."

Although his pockets, like those of any small boy, spilled string, nails, and pebbles, the Tsarevich lived in a room crammed with elaborate toys. There were "great railways with dolls in the carriages as passengers, with barriers, stations, buildings and signal boxes, flashing engines and marvelous signaling apparatus, whole battalions of tin soldiers, models of towns with church towers and domes, floating models of ships, perfectly equipped factories with doll workers and mines in exact imitation of the real thing, with miners ascending and descending." From birth, Alexis had borne the title of Hetman of all the Cossacks, and, along with his toy soldiers, toy forts, and toy guns, he had his own Cossack uniform with fur cap, boots, and dagger. In the summer, he wore a miniature uniform of a sailor of the Russian navy with "Standart," the name of the Imperial yacht, emblazoned on his cap. Unlike his sisters, who played the piano, the Tsarevich preferred the balalaika and learned to play it well. He kept a number of pets. His favorite was a silky spaniel named Joy, whose long ears dragged the ground.

The Tsarevich spent most of his time in the company of his sisters. "Luckily," wrote Pierre Gilliard, "his sisters liked playing with him. They brought into his life an element of youthful merriment that otherwise would have been sorely missed." Sometimes, by himself, he simply lay on his back staring up at the blue sky. When he was ten, Olga asked him what he was doing so quietly. "I like to think and wonder," said Alexis. "What about?" Olga persisted. "Oh, so many things," he said. "I enjoy the sun and the beauty of summer as long as I can. Who knows whether one of these days I shall not be prevented from doing it?"

When he first began to teach Alexis, the tutor found himself confronting an eight-and-a-half-year-old boy "rather tall for his age....a long, finely chiseled face, delicate features, auburn hair with a coppery glint, and large gray-blue eyes like his mother....He had a quick wit and a keen, penetrating mind. He surprised me with questions beyond his years....Those not forced to teach him habits of discipline, as I was, could quickly fall under the spell of his charm."

Even today, when regular transfusions of powerful plasma fractions make an almost normal life possible for hemophiliac boys, it is not an easy existence, either for the child or for his parents. In Alexis' day, no effective treatment had been discovered, yet Alexandra fought the disease with her whole energy, her whole soul. The birth of this child had meant everything to her. Four daughters and at last a son, the crowning of her marriage! And then the sudden, savage blow. No one seemed able to help. One by one the doctors shook their heads. The priests prayed interminably. The Empress kneeled alone on stone floors of cathedrals, churches, and chapels, begging for the health of her son. Nicholas did what he could, but his powers as autocrat had little effect in this domain. Permanently under siege, the Tsaritsa needed the understanding support of friends; if not many, then a few or at least one who could transcend all barriers of rank and share hopes and fears, talking—or even more important, listening—for hours. Alexandra herself once explained her need in a letter to an older woman. "I must have a person to myself; if I want to be my *real* self. I am not made to shine before an assembly—I have not got the easy nor the witty talk one needs for that. I like the *internal being,* and that attracts me with great force. As you know, I am of the preacher type. I want to help others in life, to help them fight their battles and bear their crosses."

Anna Vyrubova was exactly this type of person. Born Anna Taneyeva, she was twelve years younger than the Empress and came from a distinguished family. Her father, Alexander Taneyev, was both Director of the Imperial Chancellery and a noted composer. As an adolescent, Anna attended exclusive dancing classes with young Prince Felix Yussopov, the son of the wealthiest family of the Russian nobility. She had a pretty face, but she suffered chronic overweight and grew to young womanhood as a soft, doughy, submissive person whose dark eyes were always filled with an anxiety to please.

In 1901, at seventeen, Anna Taneyeva fell ill, and the Empress paid her a short visit in the hospital. It was one of many such calls that Alexandra made, but the romantic girl was overwhelmed by the gesture and conceived a passionate admiration for the twenty-nine-year-old Tsaritsa. After her recovery, Anna was invited to the palace, where Alexandra discovered that she could sing and play the piano. The two began to play duets.

An unhappy romance further strengthened the bond. Anna was being courted by Lieutenant Vyrubov, a naval officer. She was reluctant to marry, but the Empress urged her to go ahead, and she and the Tsar were witnesses at the ceremony. Within a few months, the marriage had collapsed, and Alexandra blamed herself for this misfortune. That summer—1907—Anna was invited to join the Imperial family for its annual cruise aboard the *Standart* through the Finnish fjords. Sitting on deck during the day or under lamplight in the yacht's salon at night, Anna poured her heart out. When the

At Anna Vyrubova's house at Tsarskoe Selo are (left to right) Anna, the Empress, and Lili Dehn, a close friend. There is a profusion of photographs around the room, many of which entered the Romanov family albums.

cruise ended, Alexandra declared: "I thank God for at last having sent me a true friend." Nicholas, accepting Anna, told her good-naturedly: "Now you have subscribed to come with us regularly."

From that summer, Anna Vyrubova centered her life on the Empress Alexandra and became a part of the Tsar's family. If for some reason Alexandra could not see her for a day or so, Anna pouted. At these times, the Tsaritsa teased her, calling her "our big baby" and "our little daughter." To be closer to the family, Anna moved into a small house at Tsarskoe Selo, just two hundred yards from the Alexander Palace, and her telephone was connected directly to the palace switchboard. As it was a summer house with no foundations, winter brought an icy chill rising through the floors. "When their Majesties came to tea with me in the evening," Anna wrote, "the Empress generally brought fruit and sweetmeats with her and the Emperor sometimes brought a bottle of cherry brandy. We used to sit around the table with our legs drawn up so as to avoid contact with the cold floor. Their Majesties regarded my primitive way of life from the humorous side. Sitting before the blazing hearth, we drank our tea and ate little toasted cracknels, handed around by my servant....I remember the Emperor once laughingly saying to me that, after such an evening nothing but a hot bath could make him warm again."

Most evenings, however, Anna was at the Alexander Palace. She sat with the family after dinner, joining in the puzzles, the games, the reading aloud—and the pasting of photographs into albums. In this capacity, as an almost-member of the Imperial family, Anna shared most of the adventures and trials through which the Romanovs lived during the last fateful years of their lives.

As is generally true in families, cameras were more often present and pictures most often taken during vacations. There was an annual cyclical pattern to those royal holidays. Every June the Imperial family boarded the *Standart* to cruise the fjords of Finland; in August, they went to Spala, a hunting lodge in eastern Poland, so that the Tsar could shoot stags; in September, and then again in March, they traveled to the Crimea, where the Tsar continued to work while his family rested in a summer palace overlooking the little Black Sea town of Yalta.

For the Emperor, there was no greater relaxation than the restful, sea-borne meandering along the rocky coast of Finland that he allowed himself for weeks every summer. Anchored in a lonely cove, the passengers found themselves alone in a world of sparkling blue water, red granite islands, green pine forests, and beaches of yellow sand. The vehicle for this escape into nature was a superb, black-hulled, 4,500-ton yacht, the *Standart,* which Nicholas had ordered built for himself in Denmark. Anchored in a Baltic inlet or tied up to the quay at Yalta, the *Standart* was as big as a small cruiser. She had been designed with the graceful majesty of a great sailing ship. A large bowsprit encrusted with gold leaf thrust forward from her bow, and three tall masts towered above her two white funnels. White canvas awnings stretched over polished decks lined with wicker chairs and tables. Below were a formal reception salon and drawing rooms paneled in mahogany and hung with crystal chandeliers and velvet drapes. But having made this concession to ceremonial propriety, the Empress then did all the private staterooms in chintz. Along with quarters for the Imperial suite and servants, ship's officers, crew, and a whole platoon of Marine Guards, the *Standart* also housed the members of a brass band and a balalaika orchestra.

Life aboard the yacht was informal, and the family mingled freely with the crew. Often, a group of ship's officers dined at the Imperial table, and

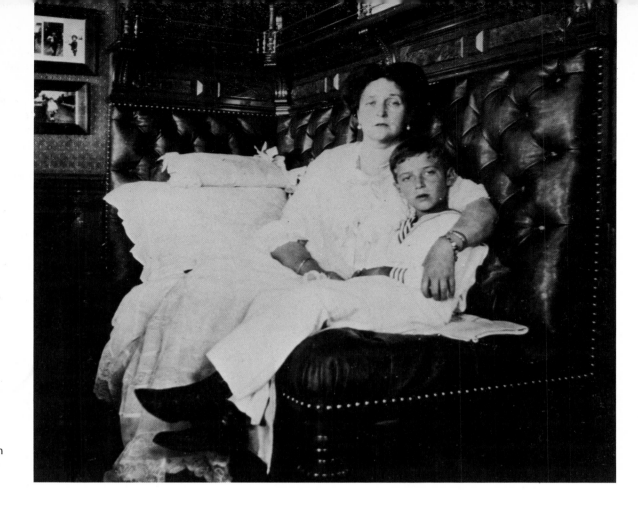

The Empress and the Tsarevich in one of the staterooms aboard the *Standart.*

bantering shipboard romances sprang up between the younger officers and the youthful Grand Duchesses. During the day, the girls wandered on deck unescorted and soon came to know most of the sailors by their first names.

At sea, Nicholas worked for two days a week, receiving and sending dispatches by the courier boats that arrived daily at the foot of the *Standart's* accommodation ladder. The rest of the time, he relaxed, rowing with his children in small boats around the yacht, walking and wading along the shore, and searching the woods for mushrooms.

Alexandra sometimes joined her family in the woods for picnics or walked along the beach, but as her sciatica worsened, she preferred to remain on the yacht, sometimes with Anna, sometimes alone, knitting, playing the piano in the salon, or simply sitting on deck watching the gulls and the sea. At teatime, the Tsar and the children returned with wildflowers, mosses, cups of mushrooms and berries, and colored rocks from the beach. Tea was served while the band played, and sometimes the Grand Duchesses and ladies-in-waiting joined the officers in a dance. Alexandra's favorite time of day was sunset when the last rays touched trees, rocks, boats, and water with golden light, and the deep male voices of the crew sang the Orthodox service of Evening Prayer. After supper, while the Emperor played billiards or smoked with his staff, the Empress read and sewed by lamplight. Well before midnight the waves had rocked them to sleep, and stewards bringing evening tea usually found the drawing room deserted.

In the courtyard of the new Marble Palace at Livadia, the Emperor confers with an aide, General Voiykov, while a regimental band plays in the background.

Of all the Imperial palaces, villas, and estates scattered across Russia, Nicholas and Alexandra preferred to be at the Livadia Palace in the Crimea. Here, in a terrain and climate similar to the Côte d'Azur, trees, shrubs, vines, and flowers bloomed as in an earthly Eden. The estate, set in the craggy hills overlooking the picturesque resort town of Yalta, was bathed in sunlight and caressed by warm breezes from the sea. Nicholas II's father, Tsar Alexander III, had built the first palace on this site, a large wooden structure decorated with traditional woodcarving, the darkness of its interior overcome with balconies giving onto the sea. In 1909 Nicholas and Alexandra decided to construct a new white limestone palace not far from the older building. Its columned courtyards and balconies were in an Italianate style that the Empress recollected from a visit to Florence before her marriage. On the exterior the structure had a light and airy appearance, which continued on the interior, where family rooms were finished in light wooden furniture and pink chintzes with mauve-colored flowers, giving the effect, Anna wrote, of a "hospitable summer home rather than a palace."

For Alexandra and Alexis, the warm days at Livadia meant recovery from illness and renewal of strength. The Empress and her son spent their mornings together, she lying in a chair on her balcony, he playing nearby with his toys. In the afternoon, the Tsaritsa went into the garden or drove her pony cart along the paths around the palace, while Alexis swam with his father in the sea. Nicholas enjoyed the water so much and considered it so healthy for his children that he had a large indoor bath constructed and filled with warm salt water, so that their daily swimming would not be affected by wind or rain or a drop in the temperature of the sea.

At Livadia, Nicholas and Alexandra could live informally. The Empress drove into Yalta to shop, something she never did in St. Petersburg or Tsarskoe Selo. Once, entering a store from a rainy street, she lowered her umbrella, allowing a stream of water to form a puddle on the floor. Annoyed, the salesman indicated a rack near the door, saying sharply, "Madame, this is for umbrellas." The Tsaritsa meekly obeyed. Only when Anna Vyrubova, who was with the Empress, addressed her in conversation as "Alexandra Feodorovna" did the astonished salesman realize who his customer was.

Nicholas spent most of his time at Livadia outdoors. Every morning, he played tennis. He made excursions with his daughters on horseback or by motorcar to neighboring villas, to the farm that supplied their table, to waterfalls and peaks in the mountains.

The Emperor of Russia was never really on vacation, and the palace at Yalta bustled with a steady stream of visitors—ministers down from St. Petersburg to report to the Tsar, local residents or guests from neighboring palaces, officers of the *Standart,* or one of the army regiments stationed in the Crimea—and unlike the procedure at Tsarskoe Selo, visitors were always invited to lunch. The children's favorite guest was the Emir of Bokhara, the ruler of an autonomous state within the Russian Empire, near the border of Afghanistan. Although he had been educated in St. Petersburg and spoke perfect Russian, the Emir followed the custom of Bokhara, and in all official conversations with the Tsar, he used an interpreter. When the Emir arrived, escorted by two of his ministers wearing long beards dyed bright red, he gave extraordinary gifts. The Tsar's sister remembered receiving "an enormous gold necklace from which, like tongues of flame, hung tassels of rubies."

The family years at Livadia ended in 1914 with the outbreak of World War I. Following the execution of the Imperial Family in 1918, and the victory

On the steps of the Catherine Palace, the Empress receives flowers from two ladies-in-waiting before an official appearance. Beside her is the little Tsarevich Alexis and Grand Duchess Tatiana. Two Cossack guards stand at attention.

"It is with poignant emotion that I recall the children as they appeared, so full of life and joy, in those distant, yet incredibly near, days before the World War and the downfall of Imperial Russia. Of the four girls, Olga was essentially Russian, altogether Romanov in her inheritance. Marie and Anastasia were also blonde types and very attractive girls. Marie had splendid eyes and rose-red cheeks…a naturally sweet disposition and a very good mind. All three of these girls were more or less the tomboy type….Anastasia, a sharp and clever child, was a very monkey for jokes, some of them almost too practical….Tatiana was almost a perfect reincarnation of her mother. Taller and slenderer than her sisters, she had the soft, refined features and the gentle, reserved manners of her English ancestry. Alexis, the only son of the Emperor and Empress…was, apart from his terrible affliction, the loveliest and most attractive of the whole family. But if he bumped his head or struck a hand or foot against a chair or table the usual result was a hideous blue swelling indicating a subcutaneous hemorrhage, frightfully painful and often enduring for days or even weeks.

"The Emperor and Empress and all the children were passionately fond of pets, especially dogs. Alexis' pets were two, a silky spaniel named Joy and a beautiful big gray cat….It was the only cat in the household and it was a privileged animal, even being allowed to sleep on Alexis' bed. There were two other dogs, Tatiana's French bull and a little King Charlie which I contributed to the menagerie. Both of these dogs went with the family to Siberia and Jimmie, the King Charles spaniel, was found shot to death in that dreadful deserted house in Ekaterinberg." A.V.

Military life and ceremony

Mass military reviews figured large and colorfully in the official life of Europe's monarchies. In Imperial Russia they were usually held in St. Petersburg on the vast parade field of Mars, but smaller regimental reviews also took place on the parade ground in front of the Catherine Palace at Tsarskoe Selo, in the presence of the Emperor and various members of his family. Each of the Grand Duchesses, as she came of age, presided over a regiment as its patroness, taking a personal interest in the welfare of the officers and sharing in the regimental esprit.

above: The Empress' balcony, seen here in a rare view of the private wing of the Alexander Palace, was the scene of many family photographs.

right: Grand Duchess Tatiana, very grown up in an elegant new suit with furs and sitting in a wicker chair on her mother's balcony.

The Empress' balcony

The Emperor in Cossack uniform, with the
Empress and Alexis on the balcony enjoying
an early spring day.

Bicycling was a favorite exercise of both father and son. Because of the danger of a fall, Alexis rode a tricycle rather than a bicycle.

Rowing and cycling

Tsar Nicholas and his family paid great attention to outdoor exercises in the course of their daily lives. The Emperor was an avid sportsman and took personal charge of the physical regimen of his son, who, despite the dangers posed by his illness, participated enthusiastically in sports and outdoor play. On a particularly fine day lessons could be put off until after lunch while everyone went outside. After the long Russian winter, a burst of sunlight in mid-April 1909 proved irresistible as the Tsar took his children out for a row on one of the canals in the park at Tsarskoe Selo. Small wood anemones, the first flowers to bloom in the early spring, can be seen everywhere. Even in their fashionable hats and long skirts, the girls row with energy just behind their father and Alexis. Grand Duchess Marie looks back at the camera (lower right).

In the winter the park at Tsarskoe Selo was an outdoor winter resort, where the whole family enjoyed hiking, sledding, skating, building snow castles, and even shoveling. The Emperor carefully demonstrated to his five-year-old son how to shovel snow, with the boy's guardian sailor Derevenko looking on.

Alexis, dressed in fur hat and long Cossack coat, energetically sets to work, with his sister Anastasia joining in the effort.

Snow shoveling

"Alexis was, apart from his affliction, the loveliest and most attractive of the whole family. As he grew older, his parents carefully explained to him the nature of his illness and impressed upon him the necessity of avoiding falls and blows. But Alexis was a child of active mind and it was almost impossible for him to avoid the very things that brought him suffering."
A.V.

Sledding

Sleighs, sleds, and toboggans have been part of the Russian winter for centuries. Once roads are snowbound, carts and carriages become useless, and vehicles equipped with runners assume great importance. Goods move to market, people visit their friends, lovers buried in furs even "go a'courtin" in sleighs and sleds. Sledding in a droshky was the favorite pastime of the Imperial family in the clear, cold days of winter. The park at Tsarskoe Selo lent itself perfectly to the long promenades where the snow flew from under the hoofs of the horses and bells rang brightly from their harnesses. Above, the Tsarevich is huddled in furs and blankets, piled on to protect him against the bitter weather. Opposite (above) the Empress sits in a small sled surrounded by her children and (below) slides down a little hill in a rare, informal moment.

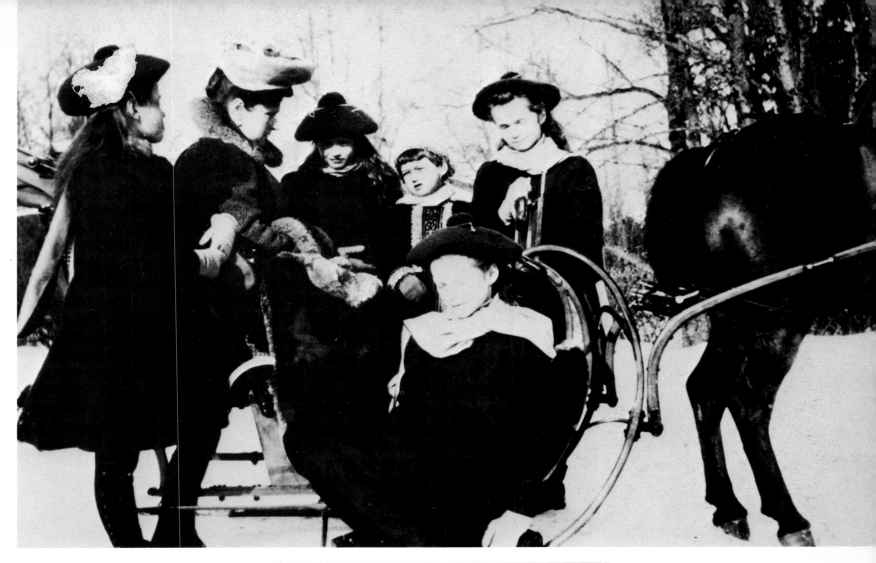

above: Skis and sleds in tow, the family group pauses for a photograph. From left to right: Anastasia, the Tsar, Grand Duchess Olga Alexandrovna (sister of the Tsar), Tatiana, Prince Serge Beloselsky, Mme. Byutsova (lady-in-waiting), Olga, and Marie.

right: The Emperor, walking stick in hand, pauses on the ice with Admiral Nilov.

Enjoying the snow

Snow falls early in Russia; in the latitude of St. Petersburg the first flakes drift to earth in October. By December the ground is covered with a deep, white blanket, constantly thickened by fresh blizzards. Winter days are short, beginning with dawn about 9 o'clock in the morning and ending at 3 P.M. when the sun goes down. All Russians, the Imperial family among them, learned to accept and even to love these frozen months. On a day when the sunlight sparkled like a shower of diamonds on the snow, children, parents, relatives, servants, and family pets all hurried out of doors to breathe the clear, cold air and to join in one of the activities or sports associated with a world of snow.

The Feodorovsky Cathedral picturesquely situated on the edge of the park. Built by the Tsar a few paces from the palace, it served as a parish church for the Imperial family and the soldiers garrisoned at Tsarskoe Selo. The exterior, completed in 1911, was a model of the Russian medieval Pskov school of architecture. In this rare view of a structure that did not survive the aftermath of the revolution, a golden Imperial eagle can be seen just above the entrance turret.

A walk in the snow-covered park accompanied by the Emperor's favorite English collie, Iman.

The mauve boudoir

"The Empress' charming boudoir was hung with mauve silk and fragrant with fresh roses and lilacs. The Empress usually lay on a low couch over which hung her favorite picture, a painting of the Holy Virgin asleep and surrounded by angels. Beside her couch stood a table, books on the lower shelf and on the upper, a confusion of family photographs, letters, telegrams and papers....The Empress never left her room before noon, it being her custom since her illness to read and write propped up on pillows on her bed." A.V.

above: The Empress writing in bed in the mauve boudoir.

right: According to Vyrubova, the opal-hued boudoir of the Empress was a lovely, quiet place, so quiet that the footsteps of the children and the sound of their pianos in the rooms above were often quite audible.

The Empress and her five children in the mauve boudoir. This photograph, taken about 1909, was published as an official portrait of the family.

above: The Empress examines a nearly completed bust of herself as the sculptor looks on.

left: In the simple schoolroom of the Alexander Palace, Pierre Gilliard, the children's Swiss tutor, gives a lesson to Grand Duchess Olga.

Children's education and activity

"Every detail of the education of her children was supervised by the Empress, who often sat with them for hours in the schoolroom. She herself taught them sewing and needlework." A.V.

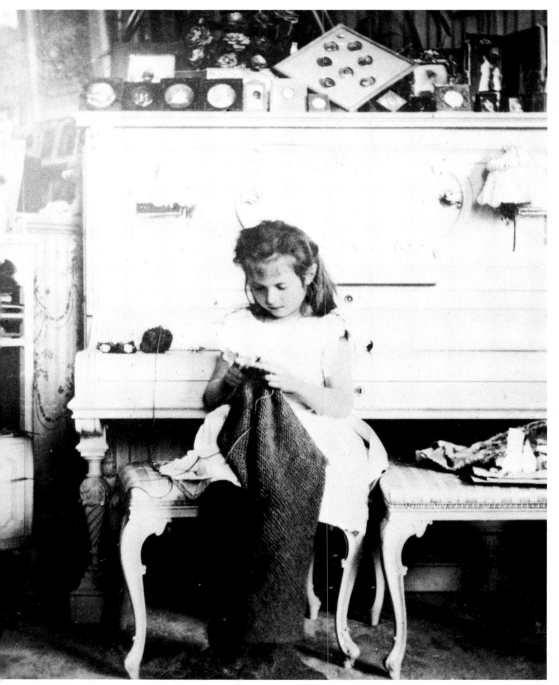

left: Seated in front of her piano in the nursery, Anastasia works on her knitting. On top of the piano is a clutter of picture frames, some of them—in diamond and square shapes— unmistakably by Fabergé.

above: The Empress, needlework in hand, shares a moment of bemusement with Olga.

Tatiana's illness and recovery

"In 1913, following the celebration of the Jubilee of the Romanovs, the three hundredth anniversary of their reign, Tatiana, who had unwisely drunk the infected water of the capital, fell ill of typhoid and could not be moved, obliging the Emperor and Empress to remain in St. Petersburg for several weeks. With her lovely brown hair cut short, we finally went back to Tsarskoe Selo, where she made good progress back to health." A.V.

right: Tatiana reading during her recuperation. On the table beside her is a collection of books, a telephone, two full-blown long-stemmed roses, and an icon, the visual call-to-prayer present in every room of an Orthodox family home.

below: The Empress sitting beside her daughter, working on her embroidery. On the bed is a knitted outfit, perhaps a recently completed project for her daughter.

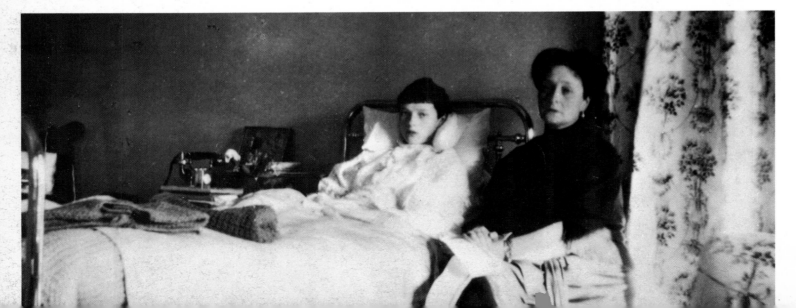

Marie, Tatiana, and Olga in 1915, dressed in mourning for the funeral of Grand Duke Constantine, the last state funeral in Imperial Russia.

Peterhof

The family spent part of every summer at Peterhof, the Imperial summer residence, begun on the Baltic by Peter the Great. While using the grand palace, designed by LeBlond in the style of Versailles, for ceremonial occasions, the family preferred to stay in the comfortable 19th-century Victorian cottage built by Nicholas I and known as the Alexandria Dacha, the Gothic Cottage, or even "the farm." Tatiana was born there in May of 1897, and the family always came to stay in the early summer just before their cruise on the Standart.

opposite: Alexis and his friends on a wagon, being pulled by the Tsarevich's sailor guard Derevenko in front of the Alexandria Dacha at Peterhof. The Empress' sisters and their children used to visit during these stays at Peterhof, and Lord Mountbatten in later years often recalled his stays there, made with his mother, Princess Victoria of Battenberg, the Empress' eldest sister.

below: Olga and Anastasia on a windowsill at the Alexandria Cottage, looking out to sea.

above: The Empress on the Baltic shore at Peterhof, with two of the sons of Grand Duke Constantine, Igor and Constantine.

below: Alexis stands astride a cannon beside the Baltic shore, quite unmindful of any danger of a fall that could bring on an attack of hemophilia.

The regiments

Military regiments played a special role in the culture of Imperial Russia. Created in the 18th century by Peter the Great, the most famous regiments wore uniforms, very colorful and formal, that immediately distinguished their officers from the rest of society, just as their special way of life did. Fundamental to every regiment was a closely knit and exclusive esprit, along with an awareness of military loyalty to the throne and to the person of the Emperor. The social life of the regiments turned on parades, Imperial dinners, and balls. A cadet's education began at a young age in the Corps des Pages or in another of the exclusive military academies, and both cadets and officers remained subjects of keen interest to romantic young women, ballerinas, and society ladies. The Empress kept her daughters away from the superficial aspects of regimental life, but officers attached to the Imperial household were always included in the family's life. Moreover, the Emperor and Empress enjoyed teasing the girls about their attraction to one or another of the young officers, with whom they were allowed an innocent romance as a normal part of growing up.

above: Two dashing officers, Groton and Samov, in their best Hussar uniforms, visiting Anna's small house at Tsarskoe Selo. The Tsar had the Hussars as his own regiment, and he kept the title of Colonel that had been bestowed on him for life before his ascent to the throne.

right: Nicholas and his son, both in Hussar uniform, on the Empress' balcony at the Alexander Palace. Alexis is unable to stand on his left leg as a result of an attack of hemophilia.

In a rare smile before the camera, the Empress with officers of the Ulan regiment, of which she was patroness. To the right of her stands the commanding officer, General Alexis Orloff, with whom Anna had once been in love. When the match was discouraged because of the difference in their ages, Anna entered a brief and disastrous marriage with another officer, Vyrubov. The union was annulled within a year. To the left of the Empress is the Emperor, who probably joined the party following a regimental lunch at the palace.

2
The Standart
Life at Sea

"When summer came…we took up our sea life on board the royal yacht the *Standart*. We cruised for two months, the Emperor frequently going ashore for tennis and other amusements, but occupied two days of each week with papers and state documents brought to him by messenger from Petrograd. The Empress and I were almost constantly together walking on shore, or sitting on deck reading, or watching the joyful play of the children, each of whom had a sailor attendant to keep them from falling overboard or otherwise suffering mishap. The special attendant of the little Alexis, Derevenko…in fact taught him to walk, and during periods of great weakness following severe attacks of his malady, carried the boy most tenderly in his arms. All of these sailors at the end of a cruise received watches and other valuable presents from the Emperor….

"In 1910 their Majesties visited Riga and other Baltic ports where they were royally welcomed, afterwards voyaging to Finnish waters where they received as guests the King and Queen of Sweden. This was an official visit, hence attended with considerable ceremony, exchange visits of the Sovereigns from yacht to warship, state dinners and receptions. At one of these dinners I sat next to the admiral of the Swedish fleet, who was much depressed because during the royal salute to the Emperor one of his sailors had accidentally been killed….

"Once, sailing through the blue Finnish fjords…a terrible thing happened, possibly an accident, but if so a very strange one, as we had on board an uncommonly able Finnish pilot. We were seated on deck at tea, the band playing, a perfectly calm sea running, when we felt a terrible shock which shook the yacht from stem to stern and sent the tea service crashing to the deck. In great alarm we sprang to our feet only to feel the yacht listing sharply to starboard. In an instant the decks were alive with sailors obeying the harsh commands of the captain, and helping the suite to look to the safety of the women and children. The fleet of torpedo boats which always surrounded the yacht made speed to the rescue and within a few minutes the children and their nurses and attendants were taken off. Not knowing the exact degree of the disaster, the Empress and I hastened to the cabins where we hurriedly tied up in sheets all the valuables we could collect. We were the last to leave the poor *Standart*, which by that time was stationary on the rocks.

"We spent the night on a small vessel, the *Asia*, the Empress taking Alexis with her in one cabin and the Emperor occupying a small cabin on deck. The little Grand Duchesses were crowded in a cabin by themselves, their nurses and attendants finding beds where they could. The ship was far from clean and I remember the Emperor, rather disheveled himself, bringing basins of water to the Empress and me in which to wash our faces and hands. We had some kind of dinner about midnight and none of us passed an especially restful night. The next day came the yacht *Alexandria* on which we spent the next two weeks. A fortnight was required to get the ill-fated *Standart* off the rocks on which she had so mysteriously been driven. From the *Alexandria* and later the *Polar Star*, to which we had been transferred, we watched the unhappy yacht being carefully removed from her captivity. We had not been very comfortable on the *Alexandria* because there was not nearly enough cabin room for our rather numerous company. The Empress occupied a cabin, the Tsarevich and his sailor another one adjoining. The four little Grand Duchesses did as well as they could in one small cabin, while the Emperor slept on a couch in the main salon. As for me, I slept in a bathroom….

"The visit to Finnish waters by the Empress Mother in 1912 was marred by no coldness or disharmony. When we went ashore for tennis, the Emperor admonished us all to play as well as we could, 'because Mama is coming.' We lunched aboard her yacht and she dined with us on the *Standart*. On the 22nd of July, which was her name day, as well as that of the little Grand Duchess Marie, she spent most of the day on the Emperor's yacht, and after luncheon I took a photograph of her sitting with her arms around the Emperor's shoulders, her two little Japanese spaniels at their feet. She made us dance for her on deck, photographing as we danced. After tea the children performed for her a little French playlet which seemed to delight her. Yet that evening at dinner I could not help noticing how her fine eyes, so kind and smiling toward most of the company, clouded slightly whenever they turned to the Emperor or the Empress. Still I must record that later, passing the open door of Alexis' cabin, I saw the Empress Mother sitting on the edge of the child's bed talking gaily and peeling an apple quite like any loving grandmother." A.V.

The family lived informally with the crew and knew many of the sailors by first name. The Tsarevich, in sailor uniform, poses here with his crew.

Sumptuous interiors
of a seagoing palace

left: The view through a porthole, looking out on the escort naval cruisers, as sketched by a guest on June 30, 1908.

below: The Empress' drawing room aboard the *Standart,* done in her favorite English chintz. Over the back of the chair on the right is a linen hand towel embroidered with a Maltese cross and "Standart" in Russian, perhaps the work of the Empress who spent many hours on board the yacht relaxing over needlework.

above: The Tsar's study aboard the *Standart,* furnished in dark leather and simple wooden furniture. An electric fan stands atop the dresser.

right: The Empress' desk in her chintz boudoir. Over it hangs a photograph of her grandmother Queen Victoria, surrounded by family pictures.

The Greatest of the Royal Yachts

The first great steam yachts were built for royalty, who used them partly to get away from pressures ashore but mainly as extravagant, private

meeting places during state visits to one another. The most splendid of all the royal yachts was Nicholas II's *Standart*. Built in Denmark and launched in 1895, the Russian Imperial yacht measured 420 feet in overall length and displaced 4,334 tons. Its engines could turn out 11,500 horsepower,

permitting a speed of nearly 22 knots. The Standart, too, was part pleasure yacht, part warship, as indicated by a warning published in 1911: "Notice to all mariners concerning seafaring regulations when the Russian Imperial yacht is in Finnish waters. Fire will be opened on all commercial shipping and all yachts—whether motor, sailing, or steam—that approach the line of guardships. All ships wishing to put to sea must seek permission not less than six hours in advance. Between sundown and sunrise, all ships underway may expect to be fired upon."

Often a group of ship's officers were invited to
dine with the Imperial family.

Crew and officials

Service on the Standart was prestigious duty for both officers and men of the yacht's crew. They bore responsibility for the lives and safety of the Emperor and his family and, in many cases, came to know these august personages—so distant from most common Russian people—as human beings. The young Grand Duchesses, for example, were addressed simply as Olga Nicolaevna or Anastasia Nicolaevna.

In addition, the Standart sailed a more interesting course than most ships of the Imperial Navy. Twice a year she made the transit from the Baltic to the Black Sea and back, a journey which took her around the Atlantic coast of Europe, through the Mediterranean and the Bosphorous. Assignment to the Standart, therefore, was a juicy plum for naval officers or ratings.

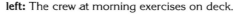

left: The crew at morning exercises on deck.

above: At the end of a cruise, all the sailors received watches and other valuable presents from the Emperor. Here they stand at attention awaiting their Tsar.

Although arrivals and departures were formal occasions, the Imperial family always managed to invest them with person warmth. Thus, each *Standart* officer greeted the Empress in the traditional manner of a Russian man to a married woman, by kissing her hand. Here, following the Empress in the receiving line are the Grand Duchesses, individually greeted with a smile and a salute.

above left: The Emperor on the deck of the *Standart* in the uniform of the British Royal Scots Greys. Nicholas II was honorary Colonel-in-Chief of that regiment, which still plays the Russian Imperial anthem at regimental parades in memory of the dead Tsar. Here, beside the Emperor is little Alexis, with Lieutenant Sablin standing at attention on the right.

left: Queen Alexandra, sister of Dowager Empress Marie, on board the *Standart* during one of the infrequent visits made by her husband, Edward VII, to his young nephew, Nicholas II.

above right: The Empress offers her hand to each officer in the receiving line. The Emperor, wearing a black mourning band, stands behind her. Dr. Botkin, later shot with the family at Ekaterinberg, salutes on the right.

right: In the uniform of a British Admiral, the Tsar meets on deck with Admiral Arseniev, also in the uniform of a British Admiral. Monarchs gave each other honorary commissions in their respective armies and navies, and they traditionally wore their foreign uniforms when visiting one another.

A game of shuffleboard on deck.

Peaceful days at sea

The *Standart* at anchor in one of the Baltic ports of call.

The Empress leaning out of a porthole.

The Emperor going down a hatch.

Launches from the *Standart* under sail off the coast of
Finland. The Imperial yacht can be seen at far left, just behind
one of the escort naval cruisers.

Officers of the Swedish entourage, one of
them carrying an umbrella, wait on deck for
the sovereigns to reappear.

Visit of the Swedish King

"In 1910 their Majesties visited Riga and other Baltic ports where they were royally welcomed, afterwards voyaging to Finnish waters where they received as guests the King and Queen of Sweden. This was an official visit, hence attended with considerable ceremony, exchange visits of the Sovereigns from yacht to warship, State dinners and receptions." A.V.

right: The King and Queen of Sweden arrive in their launch alongside the *Standart*.

below: A regatta of launches off the northern coast, viewed from the Imperial yacht.

above: Alexis, to the left of the flag, marching along the sandy shore of Finland with friends. Derevenko salutes the small battalion.

left: Alexis and friend at work in the sand. They wear sailor's hats with "Standart" emblazoned across the front. Baptismal crosses, worn by the Orthodox faithful from the time of baptism, hang on small chains around their necks.

Alexis and his friends

"Alexis, like his father, dearly loved the army and all the pageants of military display. He had every kind of toy soldier, toy guns and fortresses and with these he played for hours with his sailor companion Derevenko, or Dina as the boy called him, and with the few boy companions he was allowed." A.V.

Sometimes when the Tsar rowed ashore in the morning, he would dismiss the officers who usually accompanied him on these hikes and walk alone with his children, searching the woods for mushrooms, or wander along the beach looking for interesting stones.

Rowing and wading in the cold Baltic

left: Alexis with a lady-in-waiting just off shore.

below left: Derevenko keeping a close eye on Alexis along the rocks.

below: The Emperor, walking stick in hand, wades in water up to the top of his boots.

Tennis

When the *Standart* was anchored near the
country estate of a Russian or Finnish
nobleman, the Tsar would sometimes politely
ask if his party might use a court for tennis. He
was very fond of the sport, then new and
fashionable, and played a good game. Here
the Emperor and two officers (right) roll up
their right sleeves for a match. The ladies of
the Empress' suite often joined in these
games, even in their long dresses and hats.
Sitting on a makeshift bench (below), following
a tennis match, are the Tsar's aide-de-camp
Drenteln, Anna Vyrubova, the Emperor
smoking a cigarette, and Rodionov and Paul
Woronoff of the Naval Guard.

When it rained everyone stayed aboard. On deck in rain slickers are, from left to right, Olga, the Emperor, Marie, the Empress, and Tatiana.

The Emperor watching the crew swab down the deck.

Walks on shore

Because of her sciatica, the Empress rarely left the yacht for on-shore walks and picnics. Occasionally, however, she would join Anna and the girls, sitting in the sun on the beach while the Emperor and his suite went hiking.

top: The Emperor and his suite pause to be photographed on one of their long hikes through the pine-forested countryside of Finland. In the center is Count Grabbe, with walking stick, and to the right, holding a camera, General Orloff.

right: The Empress on one of her rare visits ashore, sits on a beach rock with Anna. Olga has been wading with them.

Nicholas retrieves a stick
from his favorite spaniel.

above: The family group, with officers and ladies-in-waiting, taken by Empress Marie aboard the *Polar Star* on her name day. To the right, an Orthodox priest. In traditional Russian culture, one's name day—the feast day of one's patron saint—is a religious celebration and more important than one's birthday, for it is a day of blessing on one's natural life. Among the Romanovs, therefore, the festivities of a name-day celebration always began with a religious service. The name day of Empress Marie, July 22, was the feast of Saint Mary Magdalene, a special holy day in Orthodox Russia. Saint Mary Magdalene, the friend of Christ, was considered the patroness of girls; thus, many women's educational institutions were named after her, including the famous Mariinsky Institute, where the Saint's feast was celebrated with a full day of festivity, opening with a Liturgy and closing with a ball.

right: After lunch on the *Standart,* the Empress' name-day continued with dancing on deck, where each of the girls chose a partner from among the young officers. Grand Duchess Olga leads the group in a polonaise. The Tsar's daughters were allowed to have their preferences for this or that handsome young officer with whom they danced, played tennis, walked, or rode. These innocent romances were a source of amusement to Nicholas and Alexandra, who enjoyed teasing the girls about any dashing officer who seemed to attract them.

The Empress' name day

"On the 22nd of July, the name-day of the Empress Mother as well as that of the little Grand Duchess Marie, she spent most of the day on the Emperor's yacht, and after lunch I took a photograph of her sitting with the Emperor, her little Japanese spaniel at their feet. She never understood, I believe, her son's preference for a quiet family life or the changed and softened manners he acquired under the influence of his wife." A.V.

below: On the right is little Anastasia in flowered hat with the ladies-in-waiting.

right: In a photograph taken by Anna Vyrubova, Empress Marie sits on the deck of the *Standart* with her son and four granddaughters Olga, Tatiana, Marie, and Anastasia. Her Japanese spaniel is at their feet.

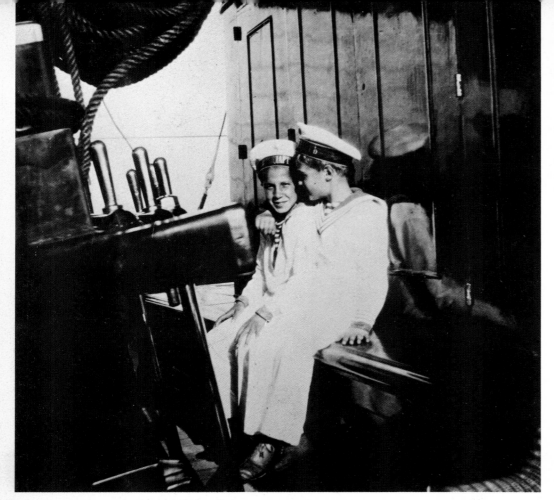

Childhood pets, friends, afflictions, and affections

"The Emperor and Empress and all the children were passionately fond of pets, especially dogs. Alexis' pets were two, a silky little spaniel named Joy and a beautiful big gray cat. It was the only cat in the household and it was a privileged animal, even being allowed to sleep on Alexis' bed." A.V.

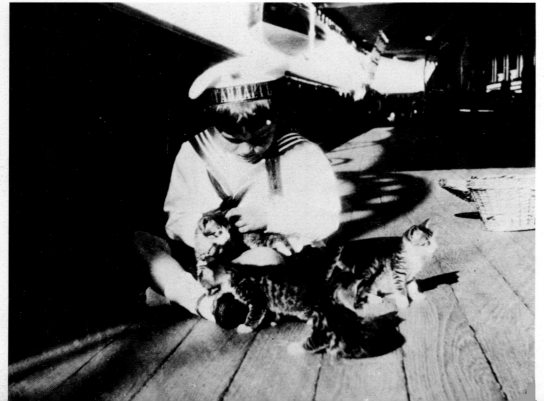

above: Alexis and a friend on the bridge of the *Standart.* The boys brought to play with Alexis were warned of the dangers of any rough activity, and all took their responsibility very seriously.

below: On deck with a basket of new kittens.

opposite left: The disease of hemophilia hung like a dark cloud over Alexis, who otherwise was a bright and sunny child. The worst pain came from bleeding into the joints. At first, the discomfort would be slight, and the limb could flex. But then, as fluid filled the socket, the effect became more severe, causing the Tsarevitch to call out: "Mama, I can't walk today." Standing on deck with his left leg flexed and his face clouded, Alexis seems to be in the early stages of an attack.

opposite far right: The Empress Alexandra endured that special kind of stress familiar only to mothers of hemophiliac sons. Not knowing when or where an attack of bleeding might start, she lived in a perpetual sense of uncertainty. Her natural reaction was to overprotect her child, but more than anything else, she remained forever ready simply to console, comfort, and suffer with him, as she seems to be doing in this photograph.

above: The girls in summer white and flowered hats on deck with their mother: Tatiana, Marie, Olga, the Empress, and Anastasia. All have adopted the current Edwardian fashion in hair, long skirts, and blouses. Permitted to indulge their own tastes in matters of clothing, the girls inclined toward simple English styles, especially for outdoor wear. In the summer, they dressed almost entirely in white.

left: Anastasia in a quiet moment standing beside Admiral Niloff on the deck of the *Standart*. Behind her, to the left, is Paul Woronoff, Countess Hendrikova, and the yacht's officers.

The Grand Duchesses

"It is with poignant emotion that I recall these innocent children as they appeared, so full of life and joy, in those distant yet incredibly near, days before the World War and the downfall of Imperial Russia."
A.V.

left: A sailor playfully restrains Marie from jumping down, while Tatiana watches.

above: Lieutenant Sablin demonstrates a telescope to Grand Duchess Olga.

Picnicking

Going ashore for a picnic constituted a great treat. Tables were set up and food brought from the yacht's kitchen, so that warm afternoons passed quickly in a bucolic setting. Like all Russians, the Imperial family often dined on the mushrooms they had gathered in the forest, the delicious harvest washed down with lots of vodka.

above: Picnicking on shore in Finland, the Emperor and Empress in the center, Olga on the left, and Anna on the right of the Emperor. Next to her is Lieutenant Sablin.

left: The Empress Alexandra on a portable chaise, dining in elegance at her own picnic table set with china and linens.

left: Alexis picking wild flowers in a Finnish field.

right: Olga reading on the beach. "Olga was perhaps the cleverest of the girls, her mind being so quick to grasp ideas, so absorbent of knowledge that she learned almost without application or close study. Had she been allowed to live her natural life she would, I believe, have become a woman of influence and distinction." A.V.

right: The Empress joins in as the Tsar holds the ladder still. Tatiana, beside her father, watches with amusement; Anna, at the bottom, is about to go next.

Men will be boys

above: All have made it to the top of the rock—the Tsar with Olga at left, Tatiana, Anastasia, a lady-in-waiting, and officers of the *Standart*.

right: The Tsar scaling an observation platform.

Tsar and Tsaritsa on board

left: Lieutenant Sablin with Grand Duke Dmitri Pavlovitch (right), cousin of the Tsar and a frequent visitor to the family. He later participated in the murder of Rasputin and was banished to Persia where he remained in exile at the time of the revolution, thereby surviving the holocaust.

above: Nicholas caught in an off-camera moment as a pensive Alexandra gazes out to sea. The sadness of this image forebodes the troubles ahead.

above left: The Empress looking out from the window of her boudoir, all the desperation of her concern for Alexis clearly apparent on her face.

above right: The Emperor, setting aside his reading, looks up at his wife, who pauses in her needlework, as Lieutenant Sablin joins them for a visit on deck.

right: The Empress and Count Benckendorff, Grand Marshall of the court, in an informal conversation. Nicholas and Alexandra maintained warm and informal relations with all of their immediate staff.

attendants, a large day room for the use of the children, and a big white hall or ballroom, seldom used.

"Below were the rooms of state, drawing rooms and dining rooms, all in white, the doors and windows opening on a marble courtyard draped with roses and vines which almost covered an antique Italian well in the center of the court. Here the Empror loved to walk and smoke after luncheon, chatting with his guests or with members of the household. The whole palace, including the rooms of state, were lightly, beautifully furnished in white wood and flowered chintzes, giving the effect of a hospitable summer home rather than a palace.

"That autumn was marked by a season of unusual gaiety in honor of the coming of age, at sixteen, of the Grand Duchess Olga, who received for the occasion a beautiful diamond ring and a necklace of diamonds and pearls. This gift of a necklace to the daughter of a Tsar when she became of age was traditional, but the expense of it to Alexandra Feodorovna, the mother of four daughters, was a matter of apprehension. Powerless to change the custom, even had she wished to do so, she tried to ease the burden on the treasury by a gradual accumulation of the jewels. By her request the necklaces, instead of being purchased outright when the young Grand Duchesses reached the age of sixteen, were collected stone by stone on their birthdays and name days. Thus at the coming out ball of the Grand Duchess Olga she wore a necklace of thirty-two superb jewels which had been accumulated for her from her babyhood.

"It was a very charming ball that marked the introduction to society of the oldest daughter of the Tsar. Flushed and fair in her first long gown, something pink and filmy and of course very smart, Olga was as excited over her debut as any other young girl. Her hair, blonde and abundant, was worn for the first time coiled up young lady fashion, and she bore herself as the central figure of the festivities with a modesty and a dignity which greatly pleased her parents. We danced in the great state dining room on the first floor, the glass doors to the courtyard thrown open, the music of the unseen orchestra floating in from the rose garden like a breath of its own wondrous fragrance. It was a perfect night, clear and warm, and the gowns and jewels of the women and the brilliant uniforms of the men made a striking spectacle under the blaze of the electric lights. The ball ended in a cotillion and a sumptuous supper served on small tables in the ballroom.

"This was a beginning of a series of festivities which the Grand Duchess Olga and a little later on her sister Tatiana enjoyed to the utmost, for they were not in the least like the conventional idea of princesses, but simple, happy, normal young girls, loving dancing and parties and all the frivolities which make youth bright and memorable. Besides the dances given at Livadia that year, large functions attended by practically everyone in the neighborhood who had Court entrée, there were a number of very brilliant balls given in honor of Olga and Tatiana after the family returned to Tsarskoe Selo....

"In relating the events of the coming of age of Olga and Tatiana I must not forget to mention affairs of almost equal consequence which occurred in the Crimea in that season of 1911. The climate of the Crimea was ideal for tubercular patients, and from her earliest married life the Empress had taken the deepest interest in the many hosptials and sanatoria which nestled among the hills, some of them almost within the confines of the Imperial estate. Before the beginning of the

The Tsar looking out over the Black Sea from the 18th-century pavilion of Oreander, one of the most beautiful of the Crimean estates near Livadia.

Crimean beauty

"In the summer of 1909 I went for the first time to Livadia, the country estate of the Imperial family in the Crimea. The vine-clad hills and valleys of the Crimea were as lovely and peaceful as the mind can picture. Imagine these valleys and plains, with their vineyards and orchards, their tall cypress trees and trailing roses sloping down to a sea as blue as the sky and as gentle as a summer day." A.V.

reign of Nicholas II and Alexandra Feodorovna these hospitals existed in numbers but they were not of the best modern type. Not satisfied with these institutions, the Empress out of her own private fortune built and equipped new and improved hospitals, and one of the first duties laid on me when I first visited the Crimea was to spend hours at a time visiting, inspecting and reporting on the condition of buildings, nursing and care of patients....

"We went to Livadia again in 1912, in 1913, and last of all in the spring and summer of 1914. We arrived in 1912 in the last week of Lent, I think the Saturday before Palm Sunday. Already the fruit trees were in full bloom and the air was warm with spring. Twice a day we attended service in the church, and on Thursday of Holy Week, a very solemn day in the Orthodox Russian calendar, their Majesties took communion, previously turning from the altar to the congregation and bowing on all sides. After this they approached the holy images and kissed them. The Empress in her white gown and cap looked beautiful if somewhat thin and frail, and it was very sweet to see the little Alexis helping his mother from her knees after each deep reverence. On Easter eve there was a procession with candles all through the courts of the palace and on Easter Sunday for two hours the soldiers, according to old custom, gathered to exchange Easter kisses with the Emperor and to receive each an Easter egg. Children from the schools came to salute in like manner the Empress. For their Majesties it was a long and fatiguing ceremony, but they carried it through with all graciousness, while the Imperial household looked on....

"In connection with the Empress' care for the tubercular patients in the Crimea there was one day every summer known as White Flower Day, and on that day every member of society, unless she had a very good excuse, went out into the town and sold white flowers for the benefit of the hospitals. It was a day especially delightful to the Empress and, as they grew old enough to participate in such duties, to all the young Grand Duchesses. The Empress and her daughters worked very hard on White Flower Day, spending practically the whole day driving and walking, mingling with the crowd and vending their flowers as enthusiastically as though their fortunes depended on selling them all. Of course they always did sell them all. The crowds surged around them eager and proud to buy a flower from their full baskets....

"Of course life in the Crimea was not all simplicity and informality. There were a great many visitors, most of them of rank too exalted to be treated with informality. I remember in particular visits of Grand Duke Ernest of Hesse, brother of the Empress, and his wife, Princess Eleanor. I remember also visits of the widowed Grand Duchess Serge, who had become a nun and was now abbess of a wonderful convent in Moscow, the House of Mary and Martha. When she visited Livadia masses were said daily in the palace church....Another memorable excursion was to the estates of Prince Oldenbourg on the coast of Caucasia. The sea that day was very rough and by the time we reached our destination the Empress was so prostrated that she could not go ashore. It was a pity because she missed what to all the others was a remarkable spectacle, a grand holiday of the Caucasians who, in their picturesque costumes, crowded down to the shore to greet their Sovereigns. The whole countryside was in festival, great bonfires burning in all the hills and on all the meadows wild music and the most fascinating of native dances.

"Such was life in the Crimea in the old, vanished days." A.V.

left: The new palace, a side view.

below: The chapel attached to the old Livadia Palace, where Anna and other members of the suite spent much time during the all-too-frequent illnesses of Alexis. "We who could do nothing for him took refuge in prayer and supplication in the little church near the palace." A.V.

opposite: Grand Duchess Olga in an arbor of glycinia.

"Flowers bloomed as though they were the very soul of the earth. Never have I seen such roses. They spread over every building in great vines as strong as ivy and scattered their rich petals over lawns and pathways in fragrance at times almost overpowering. There was another flower, the glycinia, which grew on trailing vines in grapelike clusters, deep mauve in hue, the favorite color the the Empress." A.V.

left: Anastasia and her brother in a mischievous moment as a maid prepares a tea table on one of the numerous balconies of the old Livadia Palace.

above: The Empress in one of her many moments of sadness, looking out to sea from her balcony on the old Livadia Palace.

The old palace

"The Palace as I saw it in 1909 was a large old wooden structure surrounded by balconies, the rooms dark, damp and unattractive." A.V.

right: The façade of the old Livadia Palace with its numerous balconies providing open views to the sea from the dark interior rooms.

below: The little house in English style where everyone went for tea after tennis.

Arrival at Yalta

"I shall never forget the day we landed in Yalta and the glorious drive through the bright sunshine to the Palace."
A.V.

opposite: Sun parasol in hand, the Empress strolls through a bed of roses while on a visit to the neighboring Villa Massandra, famous for its vineyard.

above: The Emperor and an officer standing beside the *Standart,* after docking in Yalta. The family usually made the thousand-mile trip from St. Petersburg by train, joining the *Standart* at Sevastapol, then traveling by sea to Yalta and continuing for several hours by carriage, later by automobile, to Livadia.

right: The girls walking along the street in Yalta with Mme. Byutsova, lady-in-waiting, and Prince Orloff, aide to the Tsar. The family enjoyed more freedom in the Crimea, where the girls were permitted to go into Yalta for outings and shopping with the Empress' ladies-in-waiting.

Excursions through the Crimea

above: The Emperor and his daughters on a drive from Livadia. From left to right, Olga, Anastasia, and Tatiana. Often the party would drive to a point and then proceed on foot.

left: The Tsar on a hike with his suite. From left, Count Grabbe, the Emperor, Prince Orloff, and Voiyekov.

"The Empress for some time had been a victim of the most alarming heart attacks which she barely concealed; eventually she consented to have the daily attention of a special physician, the devoted Dr. Botkin. He began his administration by greatly curtailing the activities of the Empress, insisting on the use of a rolling chair in the garden and a pony chaise for longer jaunts." A.V.

right: The Empress seated in her pony chaise, accompanied by her family: the Emperor and (left to right) Marie, Olga, Tatiana, and Anastasia, seated with her mother.

below: The Tsar and his daughters walking beside the pony chaise on a hike.

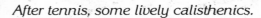

After tennis, some lively calisthenics.

opposite: Seated beside the tennis court are (left to right) Lieutenant Rodionov, Tatiana, Anastasia, the Tsar, and Olga. The Tsar and his companions all wore white shirts embroidered with the Imperial eagle.

top: The tennis group in a quiet pose: an officer, Tatiana, Olga, and the Tsar. Standing behind is Anastasia.

above and right: The scene becomes lively, after which Anastasia and an officer form a pyramid with the Tsar on top.

The Khan's visit

"We had each year many visitors. The Emir of Bokhara, a big, handsome Oriental in a long black coat and a white turban glittering with diamonds and rubies, sometimes came to lunch. He seemed intensely interested in the comparative simplicity of Russian royal customs and when he departed for his own land he distributed presents in true Arabian nights profusion, costly diamonds and rubies to their Majesties and to the suite, orders decorations set with jewels." A.V.

left: The arrival of the Emir of Bokhara at Livadia.

above: The Emir and Count Benckendorff exchange bows in greeting.

below: The Emir, his white turban barely visible, departs in a carriage. In the foreground is Grand Duchess Marie.

opposite: The Empress shares a joke with officers of her Ulan regiment.

The charity bazaar

"The climate of the Crimea was ideal for tubercular patients, and from her early married life the Empress had taken the deepest interest in the many hospitals and sanatoria which nestled among the hills, some of them almost within the confines of the Imperial estate. One of the first duties laid on me when I first visited the Crimea was to spend hours at a time visiting, inspecting and reporting on the condition of buildings, nursing and care of patients. The Empress, out of her own private fortune, built and equipped new and improved hospitals.

One of each summer's activities, when the family visited the Crimea, was a bazaar or other entertainment for the benefit of the care of those patients too poor to pay for the best food and nursing. I remember four great bazaars organized and managed by the Empress—the first held in 1911 and the others in 1912, 1913 and 1914. From the opening day the Empress always presided over her own table, disposing of fine needlework, embroidery and art objects with energy and enthusiasm. The crowds at her booth were enormous, the people pressing forward almost frenziedly to touch her hand, her sleeve, her dress. The great mass of the Russian people loved and were loyal to their sovereigns. No one who knew them at all can ever forget that." A.V.

above: With the Emperor's portrait presiding over the sale, everything is ready for the great event.

left: The Empress selling wares at her table. The whole family participated in the bazaar, the girls selling at other tables and the Emperor and Alexis, along with officers from the *Standart*, lending a hand wherever needed.

opposite: The crowded room where the Empress circulates with her daughters and ladies-in-waiting.

Sports for the children

"Life at Livadia in 1909 and in after years was simple and informal. We walked, rode, bathed in the sea and generally led a healthful country life." A.V.

opposite: Wading in the sea—Tatiana and Olga with Anna, her camera in hand. Swimsuits had not yet come into vogue!

above: Tatiana and Olga pose side-saddle on their ponies. As officers of regiments, they had to develop their equestrian skills.

right: Bathing in the fresh-water pool that the Tsar had had constructed at Livadia. Anna in the middle, surrounded by the girls.

above left: Pierre Gilliard, the children's Swiss tutor, giving lessons to Olga and Tatiana on the sun-drenched terrace at Livadia.

left: After taking Holy Communion, the family break their fast with a light meal in the Empress' Art Nouveau drawing room. In the Orthodox Church, no food or drink may be taken before receiving the sacrament.

above: The Emperor and Empress on top of Ai Petri ("Saint Peter"), the Tartar name for that mountain peak.

opposite: A visit in May 1916 to the Karaim, an ancient Christian religious group in the Crimea. Worshiping in synagogues, the sect consisted of a strange mixture of Christians and Jews, whose shared traditions went back to the days of the decaying Roman Empire, when Judaism and Christianity were trying to unite in one faith. The head of the Karaim, a black-bearded Patriarch named Gahan, walks beside the Emperor, accompanied by Alexis and one of the Grand Duchesses. Ladies-in-waiting and gentlemen of the court line the route.

4
Spala
Polish Retreat: The Imperial Hunting Lodge

"In the autumn of 1912 the family went to Skernivizi, their Polish estate, in order to indulge the Emperor's love for big-game hunting.... A telegram from the Empress to me at Tsarskoe Selo conveyed the disquieting news that Alexis, in jumping into a boat, had injured himself and was now in a serious condition. The child had been removed from Skernivizi to Spala, a smaller Polish estate near Warsaw, to which I was summoned. I was met by one of the Imperial carriages in Warsaw and was driven to Spala. Driving for nearly an hour through deep woods and over a heavy, sandy road I reached my destination, a small wooden house, something like a country inn, in which the suite was lodged. Two rooms had been set aside for me and my maid, and here I found Olga and Tatiana waiting to help me get settled. Their mother, they said, was expecting me, and without any loss of time I went with them to the palace.

"I found the Empress greatly agitated. The boy was temporarily improved but was still too delicate to be taken back to Tsarskoe Selo. Meanwhile the family lived in one of the dampest, gloomiest palaces I have ever seen. It was really a large wooden villa, very badly planned as far as light and sunshine were concerned. The large dining room on the ground floor was so dark that the electric lights had to be kept on all day. Upstairs to the right of a long corridor were the rooms of the Emperor and Empress, her sitting room in bright English chintzes being one of the few cheerful spots in the house. Here we usually spent our evenings. The bedrooms and dressing rooms were too dark for comfort, but the Emperor's study, also on the right of the corridor, was fairly bright.

"As long as the health of little Alexis continued fairly satisfactory the Emperor and his suite went stag hunting daily in the forests of the estate. Every evening after dinner the slain stags were brought to the front of the palace and laid out for inspection on the grass. The huntsmen with their flaring torches and winding horns standing over the day's bag made a very picturesque spectacle. The Emperor and his suite and most of the household used to enjoy going out after dinner to enjoy this fine sight.... The corridors and apartments of the palace were adorned with many trophies of the chase.

"I enjoyed the beautiful park which surrounded the palace, and the rapid little river Pilitsa that flowed through it. There was one leafy path through which I often walked in the mornings with the Emperor. This was called the Road of Mushrooms because it ended in a wonderful mushroom bench. The whole place was so remote and peaceful that I deeply sympathized with their Majesties' irritation that even there they could never stir abroad without being haunted by the police guard.

"Although Alexis' illness was believed to have taken a favorable turn and he was even beginning to walk a little about the house and gardens, I found him pale and decidedly out of condition. He occasionally complained of pain, but the doctors were unable to discover any actual injury. One day the Empress took the child for a drive and before we had gone very far we saw that indeed he was very ill. He cried out with pain in his back and stomach, and the Empress, terribly frightened, gave the order to return to the palace. That return drive stands out in my mind as an experience of horror. Every movement of the carriage, every rough place in the road, caused the child the most exquisite torture, and by the time we reached home he was almost unconscious with pain. The next weeks were endless torment to the boy and to all of us who had to listen to his constant cries of pain. For fully eleven days these dreadful sounds filled the corridors outside his room, and those of us who were obliged to approach had often to stop our ears with our hands in order to go about our duties. During the entire time the Empress never undressed, never went to bed, rarely even lay down for an hour's rest. Hour after hour she sat beside the bed where the half-conscious child lay huddled on one side, his left leg drawn up so sharply that for nearly a year afterwards he could not straighten it out. His face was absolutely bloodless, drawn and seamed with suffering, while his almost expressionless eyes rolled back in his head. Once when the Emperor came into the room, seeing his boy in this agony and hearing his faint screams of pain, the poor father's courage completely gave way and he rushed, weeping bitterly, to his study. Both the parents believed the child dying, and Alexis himself, in one of his rare moments of consciousness, said to his mother: 'When I am dead build me a little monument of stones in the wood.'

"The family's most trusted physicians....were in charge of the case and after the first consultations declared the Tsarevich's condition hopeless. The hemorrhage of the stomach from which he was suffering seemed liable to turn into an abscess which could at any moment prove fatal....One evening after dinner when we were sitting very quietly in the Empress' boudoir, Princess Henry of Prussia, who had come to be with her sister in her trouble, appeared in the doorway very white and agitated and begged the members of the suite to retire as the child's condition was desperate. At eleven o'clock the Emperor and Empress entered the room, despair written on their faces. Still the Empress declared that she could not believe that God had abandoned them.... As a matter of fact the turning point came a few days later, the pain subsided, and the boy lay wasted and utterly spent, but alive.

above: The simple wooden façade of the "palace" at Spala.

right: There being no church on the Spala estate, Nicholas and Alexandra had a large green tent erected in the garden to serve as a chapel during the illness of Alexis. Morning and night a priest officiated here at a small portable altar, leading prayers for the recovery of the Tsarevich twice a day.

"Curiously enough there was no church on this Polish estate, but during the illness of the Tsarevich a chapel was installed in a large green tent in the garden. A new confessor, Father Alexander, celebrated Mass and after the first celebration he walked in solemn procession from the altar to the sickroom bearing holy communion for the sick boy...

"The convalescence of Alexis was slow and wearisome. His nurse Marie Vechniakoff, had grown so hysterical with fatigue that she had to be relieved, while the Empress was so exhausted that she could hardly move from room to room. The young Grand Duchesses were tireless in their devotion to the poor invalid, as was also M. Gilliard, who read to him and diverted him hours on end. Gradually the distracted household assumed a more normal aspect. The Emperor, in Cossack uniform, began once more to entertain the officers of his Varsovie Lancers, commanded by a splendid soldier, General Mannerheim, of whom the world has heard much. As Alexis' health continued to improve there was even a little shooting, and a great deal of tennis which the girls, after their long confinement to the house, greatly enjoyed. All of us began to be happy again." A.V.

The Emperor stands beside his shoot of the day. The slain stag, laid out on the front lawn, is tagged with the crowned monogram of the Emperor: N II ("H II" in Russian).

"The Emperor and his suite went stag hunting daily in the forests of the estate. Every evening after dinner the slain stags were brought to the front of the palace and laid out for inspection on the grass. The Emperor and his suite and most of the household used to enjoy going out after dinner to enjoy this fine sight." A.V.

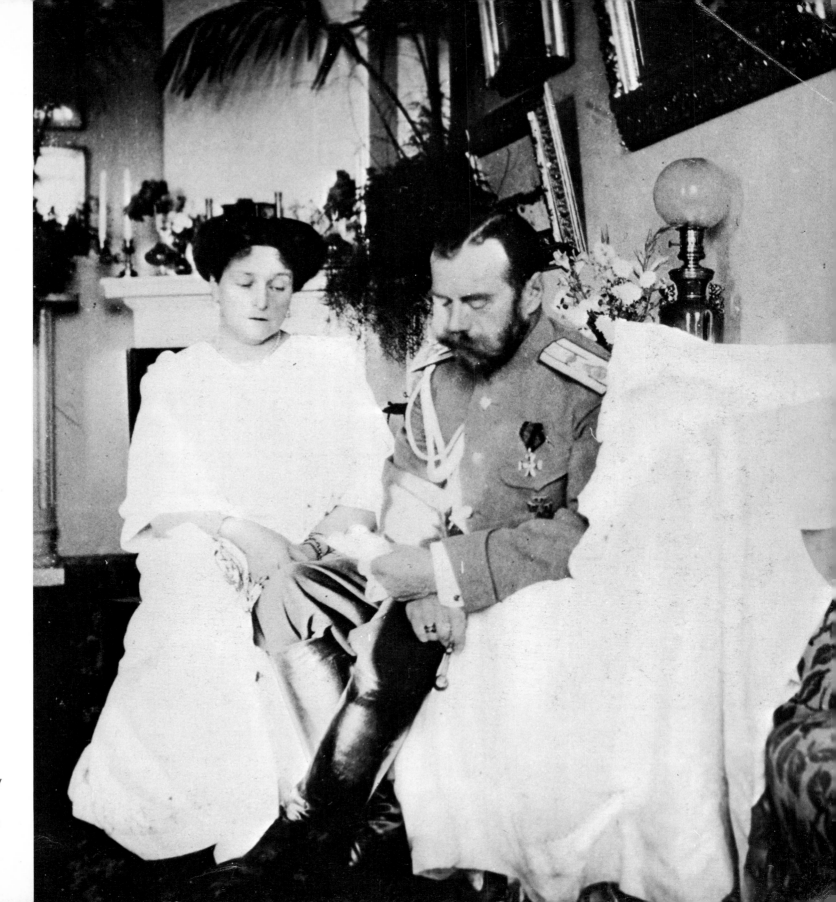

In the Empress' drawing room, Nicholas and Alexandra anxiously look over some of the letters and telegrams that began pouring in from all over the country as news of the Tsarevich's illness became known.

opposite: The Tsar sitting on the steps of the palace with officers of the suite. Next to him is Prince Orloff. Note the varied uniforms of the different regiments.

above: The Emperor at ease with officers on the front lawn of the palace.

right: The Emperor meeting officers at Spala. To the left in Cossack uniform is Count Grabbe, head of the Tsar's Cossacks known as the *Konvoi*. Official routine proceeded normally during the illness of the Tsarevich, the better to avoid drawing attention to the boy's serious condition. Everyone took their cue from the Tsar and Tsaritsa and behaved as if the danger had not arisen.

far left: Local children in Polish national costume. Many of the peasants from the surrounding area came when religious services were held in the open forest.

left: As Alexis' condition finally turned for the better, the court began to show signs of relief. The Emperor smiles as he holds up a tennis racquet.

Life returns to normal. Marie and Anastasia, tennis racquets in hand.

The Empress out for a walk with her sister, Princess Irene of Prussia, who had come to be with her. The Princess was still in mourning for her own little son, who had died of the same incurable disease that afflicted the Tsarevich. Anna recalled how "she spoke to me with emotion of the child, to whom she had been deeply attached."

113

The Tsar's official declaration of war at the Winter Palace on July 20, 1914, reprinted on a postcard for general distribution.

5
World War I
End of a Dynasty

"Nineteen fourteen, that year of fate for all the world, but more than all for my poor country, began its course in Russia, as elsewhere, in apparent peace and tranquillity…. Then came the day of mobilization, the same kind of a day of wild excitement, waving street crowds, weeping women and children, heartrending scenes of parting, that all the warring countries saw and ever will remember. After watching hours of these dreadful scenes in the streets of Peterhof I went to my evening duties with the Empress…. 'War,' she murmured breathlessly…. 'This is the end of everything….'

"The state visit of their Majesties to Petrograd soon after the declaration really seemed to justify the Emperor's belief that the war would arouse the national spirit, so long latent in the Russian people. Never again do I expect to behold such a sight as the streets of Petrograd presented on that day…. The streets were almost literally impassable, and the Imperial motor cars, moving at snail's pace from quay to palace through that frenzied sea of people cheering, singing the national anthem, calling down blessings on the Emperor, was something that will live forever in the memories of all who witnessed it. The Imperial cortege was able, thanks to the police, to reach the Winter Palace at last, but many of the suite were halted by the crowds at the entrance to the great square in front of the palace and had to enter at a side door….

"Inside the palace the crowd was relatively as great as that on the outside. Apparently every man and woman who had the right to appear at Court were massed in the corridors, the staircases and the state apartments. Slowly their Majesties made their way to the great Salle de Nicholas, the largest hall in the palace, and there for several hours they stood receiving the most extraordinary tokens of homage from thousands of officials, ministers and members of the *noblesse*, both men and women. Te Deums were sung, cheers and acclamations arose, and as the Emperor and Empress moved slowly through the crowds, men and women threw themselves on their knees, kissing the hands of their Sovereigns with tears and fervent expressions of loyalty. Standing with others of the suite in the Halle de Concert, I watched this remarkable scene, and I listened to the historic speech of the Emperor which ended with the assurance that never would there be an end to Russian military effort until the last German was expelled from the beloved soil. From the Salle de Nicholas, the Sovereigns passed to a balcony overlooking the great square. There with the Tsarevich at their side they faced the wildly exulting people who with one accord dropped to their knees with mute gestures of love and obedience. Then as countless flags waved and dipped there arose from the lips and hearts of that vast assembly the moving strains of our great hymn: 'God save the Tsar.'

The Tsar talking with Grand Duke
Nicholas Nicholaevitch, appointed
General-in-Chief of the Russian
armies until the Tsar himself took
command in September of 1915.

Crowds in front of the Winter Palace on the day the Tsar declared war.

"Thus in a passion of renewed love and patriotism began in Russia the war of 1914. That same day the family returning to Peterhof, the Emperor almost immediately leaving for the casernes to bid farewell to regiments leaving for the front. As for the Empress, she became overnight a changed being. Every bodily ill and weakness forgotten, she began at once an extensive plan for a system of hospitals and sanitary trains for the dreadful roll of wounded which she knew must begin with the first battle. Her projected chain of hospitals and sanitary centers reached from Petrograd and Moscow to Kharkoff and Odessa in the extreme south of Russia. The center of her personal activity was fixed in a large group of evacuation hospitals in and around Tsarskoe Selo, and there I joined the Empress.... The Empress, her two older daughters, and myself immediately enrolled under a competent woman surgeon, Dr. Gedroiz, as student nurses, spending two hours every afternoon

under theoretical instruction, and the entire hours of the morning in ward work in the hospitals.... Arriving at the hospital shortly after nine in the morning we went directly to the receiving wards where the men were brought in after having first aid treatment in the trenches and field hospitals. They had travelled far and were usually dirty as well as bloodstained and suffering. Our hands scrubbed in antiseptic solutions, we began the work of washing, cleaning and bandaging maimed bodies, mangled faces, blinded eyes, all the indescribable mutilations of what is called civilized warfare. This we did under the orders and the direction of trained nurses. As we became accustomed to the work, and as both the Empress and Tatiana had extraordinary ability as nurses, we were given more important work.... I have seen the Empress of Russia in the operating room of a hospital holding ether cones, handling sterilized instruments, assisting in the most difficult operations, taking from the

The Tsar on the balcony of the Winter Palace following the Liturgy and his solemn oath to defend the motherland.

hands of the busy surgeons amputated legs and arms, removing bloody and even vermin infected dressings, enduring all the sights and smells and agonies of that most dreadful of all places, a military hospital in the midst of war. She did her work with the humility and the gentle tirelessness of one dedicated by God to a life of ministration. Tatiana was almost as skillful and quite as devoted as her mother, and complained only that on account of her youth she was spared some of the more trying cases. The Empress was spared nothing, nor did she wish to be. I think I never saw her happier than on the day, at the end of our two months' intensive training, she marched at the head of the procession of nurses to receive the red cross and the diploma of a certified war nurse.

"From that time on our days were literally devoted to toil. We rose at seven in the morning and very often it was an hour or two after midnight before we sought our beds. The Empress, after a morning in the operating room of one hospital, snatched a hasty luncheon and spent the rest of the day in a round of inspection of other hospitals. Every morning early I met her in the little Church of Our Lady of Znamenie....driving afterwards to the hospitals. On the days when the sanitary trains arrived with their ghastly loads of wounded we often worked from nine until three without stopping for food or rest. The Empress literally shirked nothing. Sometimes when an unfortunate soldier was told by the surgeons that he must suffer an amputation or undergo an operation which might be fatal, he turned in his bed calling out her name in anguished appeal.... Were the man an officer or a simple peasant boy, she always answered the appeal. With her arm under his head she would speak words of comfort and encouragement, praying with him while preparations for the operation were in progress, her own hands assisting in the merciful work of anesthesia." A.V.

After the Tsar had assumed command of the army, he spent a great deal of time at Stavka, the Russian military headquarters near Mogilev. He often took Alexis with him, perhaps with the idea of educating the boy for his future role, something his own father had not adequately done for him. The Tsarevich presides over the table where officers and the allied military commanders have gathered for luncheon. The Tsar is third from the left

right: The Empress and her daughters occasionally visited Stavka, making the trip from Tsarskoe Selo on the Imperial train. Here, in one of the comfortable drawing rooms on the train, the family group includes (from left to right) Grand Duke Dimitri Pavlovitch, the Tsar, the Tsaritsa, Grand Duke Michael (the Tsar's brother), Tatiana, and Olga, with Anastasia and Marie seated on the floor.

below: The Imperial family with officers of the *Konvoi,* the Tsar's regiment of Cossacks.

below: A young doctor stands at the entrance to one of the Empress' infirmaries. A recuperating officer is at the door behind him.

right: The Empress at Peterhof in her nursing habit, carrying a bouquet of roses from the gardens there.

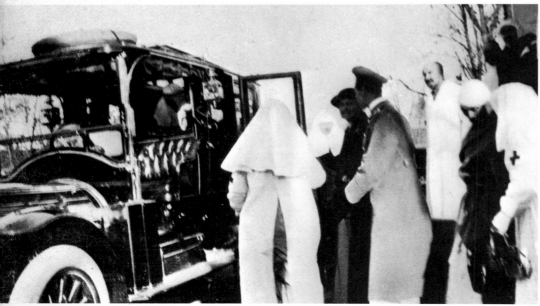

left: The Empress and her daughters in their habits as nursing sisters leave the hospital for the drive back to the Alexander Palace. People waited daily along the route to see the motor car pass. Gradually the girls recognized the same people each day and greeted them with smiles and waving.

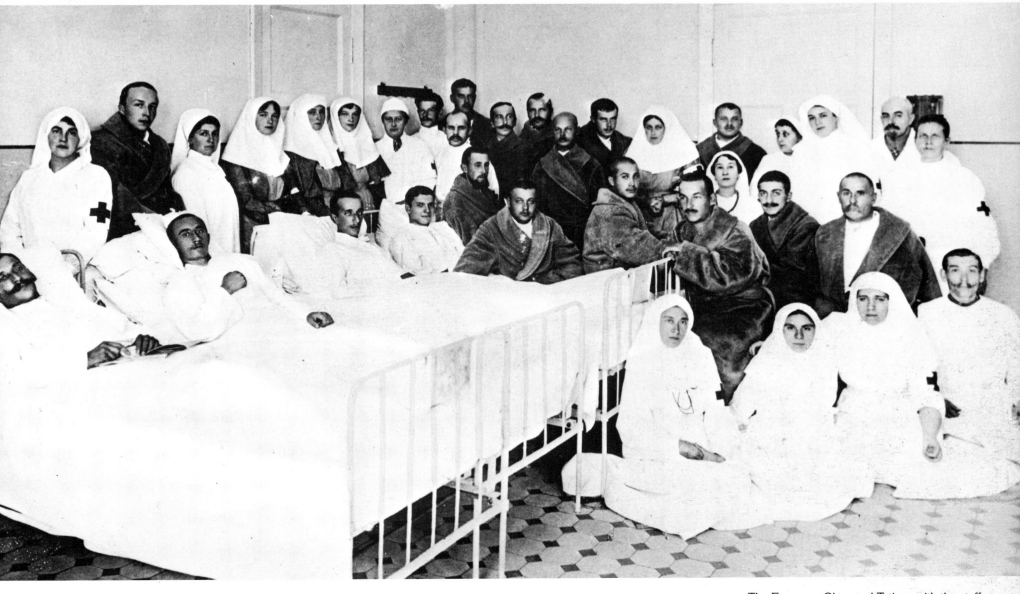

The Empress, Olga, and Tatiana with the staff of hospital nurses in a ward. Anna stands near the door on the right.

Hospital scenes

"The war of 1914 began in Russia in a passion of renewed love and patriotism. The Empress became, overnight, a changed being. Every bodily ill and weakness forgotten, she began at once an extensive plan for a system of hospitals and sanitary trains for the dreadful roll of wounded which she knew must begin with the first battle. The center of her personal activity was fixed in a large group of evacuation hospitals in and around Tsarskoe Selo, and there, after bidding farewell to my only brother, who immediately left for the front, I joined the Empress."
A.V.

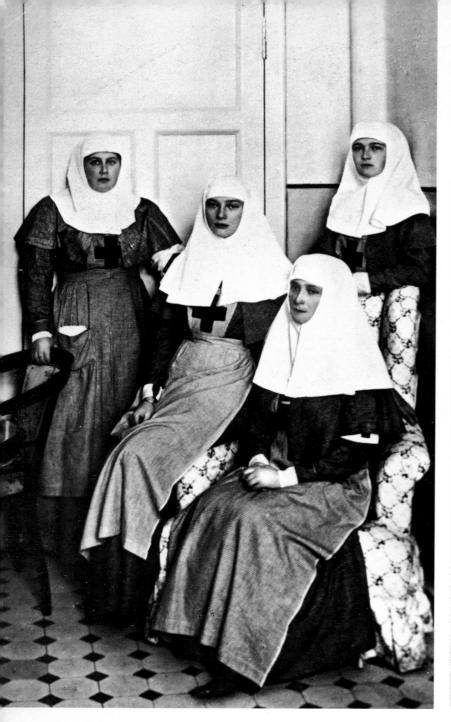

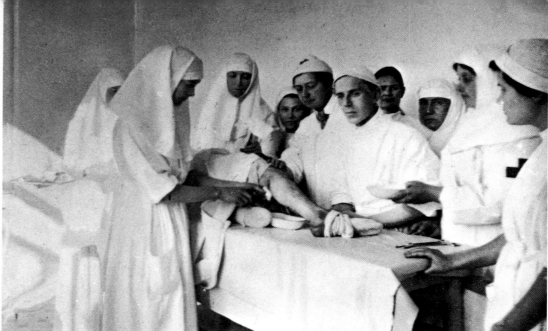

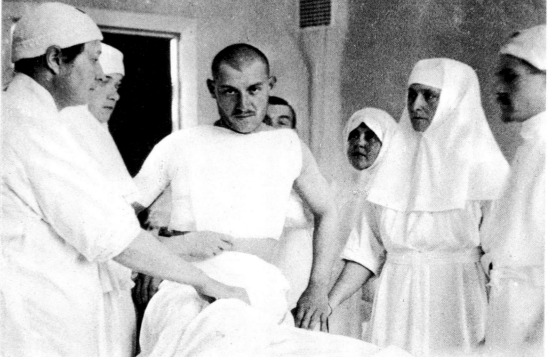

left: An official portrait of the Imperial nurses—the Empress, seated, with Tatiana at her left, Olga standing behind her. Anna stands near the door.

top: Tatiana dressing a wound in the hospital operating room.

above: The Empress taking the hand of a wounded soldier in pain.

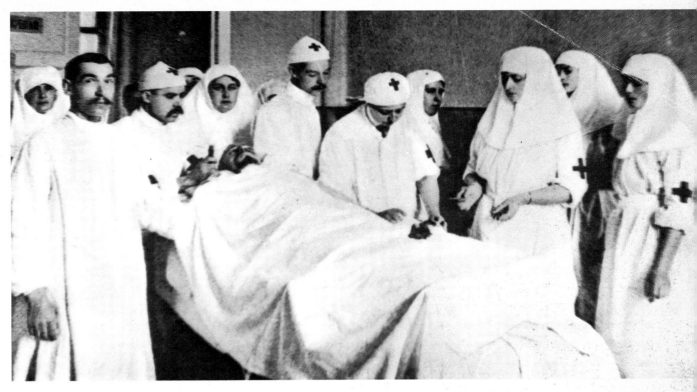

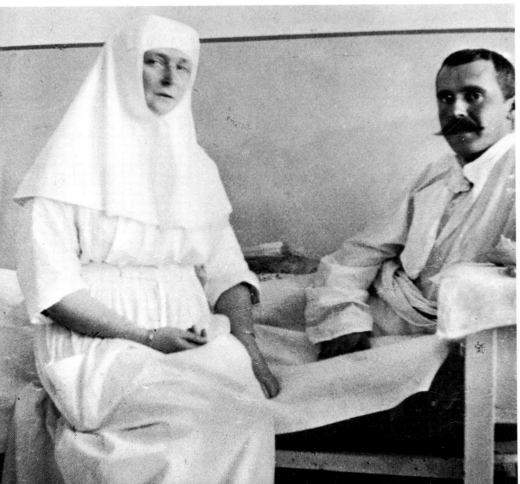

left: The Empress sits on the bed of a young officer in recuperation.

above: The Empress assists a surgeon during an operation. Olga, Tatiana, and Anna stand behind the operating table.

opposite: In March 1917, following the abdication of the Tsar and his brother Grand Duke Michael, the Imperial family were put under house arrest at Tsarskoe Selo. In the early summer, unaware that they would soon be transferred to Siberia, they began to plant a vegetable garden in the park outside the Alexander Palace. In this picture, Tatiana carries a litter of ground cover with Countess Nastya Hendrikova, who was later shot by the Bolsheviks for refusing to renounce the Imperial family. The Tsar stands with his back to the camera, shovel in hand.

right: Nicholas and his daughters at Tobolsk. This photograph of the then former Emperor and his daughters, Olga, Marie, and Tatiana in the compound of the governor's house in Tobolsk, was smuggled to Anna in Petrograd along with letters from the Empress describing the conditions of their exile.

below: The former Tsar and his son, sawing wood in the yard of the governor's house at Tobolsk where the family spent eight months in captivity. The Tsarevich had grown taller as he approached the age of fourteen.

Щедръ и млтивъ Гдъ долготерпѣливъ и многомлтивъ. Не до конца̀ прогнѣвлетсѧ нижѐ въ вѣкъ враждꙋетъ Млⷭть же Гдⷩѧ ѿ вѣка й до вѣка на боѧщихсѧ Егѡ҆.

As conditions worsened all around them, the Imperial family realized that their lives would eventually be taken. "What we are doing is preparing our souls for the Kingdom of Heaven," the Empress wrote to Anna in one of her smuggled letters. On this prayer card, also painted at Tobolsk in 1918, she copied a troparion *from the Orthodox Requiem Service (the panikhida):* "O Thou who, with wisdom profound, mercifully orderest all things, and who givest that which is expedient unto all men, Thou Only Creator; Give rest, O Lord, to the souls of Thy servants who have fallen asleep; for they have set their hope on Thee, our Maker, the Author of our being, and our God."

During all this time the family responded with extraordinary calm and courage toward everyone around them, and with the spiritual strength of Christian martyrs. Grand Duchess Olga wrote in one of her letters from Tobolsk: "Father asks to have it passed on to all who have remained loyal to him and to those on whom they might have influence, that they not avenge him; he has forgiven and prays for everyone; and not to avenge themselves, but to remember that the evil which is now in the world will become yet more powerful, and that it is not evil which conquers evil, but only love...."

Prayer card painted by the Empress at Tobolsk in 1918. Artistically written in old Church Slavonic and decorated with Art Nouveau designs and a swastika, a favorite symbol of the Empress and an ancient Eastern symbol of health and prosperity also found in the catacombs of the early Christians, is a verse from Psalm 103: 8–9: "The Lord is compassionate and gracious, long suffering and forever constant; he will not always be the accuser or nurse his anger for all time."